THE
AMBASSADOR'S
DAUGHTER

AN AUTOBIOGRAPHY

DEBORAH KORRY SIMCOX

Praise for

THE AMBASSADOR'S DAUGHTER

Fate gave me the role of telling the true story of legendary journalist and Ambassador Edward M. Korry, when no other reporter would. The autobiography of his daughter Deborah is a story told with amazing courage, and adds even more to the understanding of man, his family and a remarkable daughter.

- **Joseph Trento, Award winning investigative journalist and author of 8 books including *America and the Islamic Bomb* and *Unsafe at any Altitude.***

Those of us who have served in the diplomatic world will recognize the complex and unsettled life Deborah Korry lived as daughter of a United States ambassador. What she did with that life as an adult is a tribute to her own unique independence and courage. Well done, Deborah!

- **Cristian Maquieira, a Chilean diplomat for 42 years, served as Deputy Ambassador to the UN and Chilean Ambassador to Paraguay. Currently he is a professor at the Diplomatic Academy in Santiago Chile.**

I remember Deborah Korry as a talented, insightful, and highly valued employee at our firm in the 1990s, and she remains a trusted and valued friend. However, until I read her book, I had no inkling of the richness and variety of her past life as an ambassador's daughter, nor the challenges she faced to become the person she is today. The book is riveting.

- Bob Byrne was CEO of the actuarial consulting firm Kwasha Lipton and co-inventor of the first cash balance pension plan. He is currently a Senior Consultant at Willis Towers Watson, a global advisory firm.

Some will wonder how much there is to learn about the neighbor across the fence! As next-door neighbor to Deborah for a number of years, we have enjoyed many conversations in our native French, many of them at our frequent backyard barbecues. While I knew she was an ambassador's daughter, the Deborah I admire is a kind woman who combines lightness of spirit with a down to earth frankness that is unusual and refreshing. Her writing on Paris revived my childhood, and although her early life may sound like a fairy tale, it is filled with harsh reality mixed with the lessons of forgiving, listening, understanding and compassion. I am glad to say this is the Deborah who shines through the pages of her enjoyable and revealing book, written by a fully aware and amazing woman. She is, above all, my dear friend.

- Florian Bellanger, award-winning Pastry Chef and competition judge on the Food Network.

The Ambassador's Daughter/ Deborah Korry Simcox -- 1st ed.

ISBN 978-0-692-06080-3 Print Edition

ISBN 978-0-692-06081-0 Ebook Edition

Contents

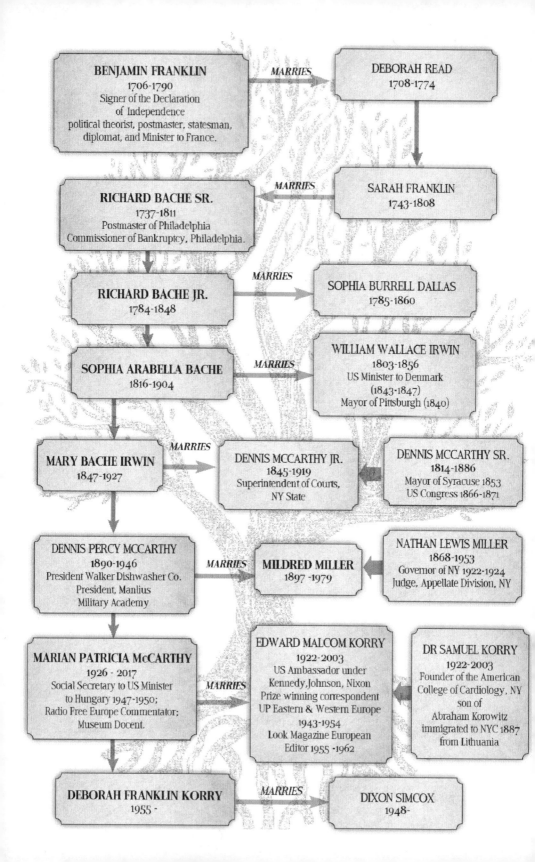

"Either write something worth reading
or do something worth writing."

– Benjamin Franklin

(1706-1790)

My grandfather, to the seventh generation.

ENDINGS AND BEGINNINGS

Christmas Eve 2000 was the last time I saw my father in the full vigor of life. Always the ultimate diplomat, journalist, presidential advisor, and foreign policy expert, now he stood at his kitchen stove, stirring something in a pot. Cooking was a passion he took up only in his 70s, but he did it with the same intensity and passion he did everything else in life, except—perhaps—reach out to me.

"Hello, Papa," I said, setting down my bags. He half turned toward me, still stirring. If he had any idea that I had traveled several hundred miles and altered my holiday plans just to visit him in North Carolina, he did not let on.

"Nice to see you," he said, and turned back to his cooking.

This was my father—an enigma, a stranger, a man always in control. He spent his life doling out equal parts of suave statesman and loving husband, and he was known as a kind, understanding, and compassionate man to all. As far as I know, I was his only disappointment who was not worthy of his affection. Yet I adored him.

Papa's remoteness was perfectly reflected in my mother as well. Earlier that day, I had called to say I was celebrating Christmas with my husband, Dixon, and his family in nearby Georgia.

"Hi, Mummy, I'm going to surprise you," I said. "I'm only about three hours away, and I thought I'd come by and see you both for Christmas."

"Oh, what do you mean?" she said, her voice shrill with anxiety. "This isn't a good time for you to come!"

"Well, I'll just stop by for twenty minutes or something," I said.

My mother said, "Well, your father is working on his book and we didn't make plans for you to come. This really isn't an ideal time."

****

My father, Edward Malcolm Korry, never finished his book (though my brother Ted has pledged to). Given my father's skills as a writer, I have no doubt that one day his book will be highly regarded as a resource and history of the mid-twentieth century American politics, foreign policy, and journalism. He experienced it all, both as a leader and as a participant. Over the course of his eighty years, he was at the center of government and American history: first as an overseas journalist and editor—and then as an ambassador and policy advisor to three presidents: Kennedy, Johnson, and Nixon.

The first, John F. Kennedy, appointed him ambassador to Ethiopia: a crucial international assignment under the powerful and charismatic Emperor Haile Selassie. Later, Lyndon Johnson named him ambassador to Chile, a post which came with all the messy intrigues of that politically restless country, and which eventually embittered my father to public service.

But through all kinds of political weather, when it came to public service we Korrys' plunged in as a family enterprise. We liked to joke that instead of a wall of family photos (Mummy, Papa, and the children), the photos displayed in our living room were snapshots of the emperor of Ethiopia, the president of Chile, and various assortments of VIPs.

Even the family photos were a cut above the backyard barbecue

THE AMBASSADOR'S DAUGHTER • 3

variety. One of them, taken in the Oval Office, shows our family clustered informally around President Kennedy, who is looking mischievous and relaxed, as if he's in the middle of telling us a good joke. When it came to playing the role of the perfect family, we did it well.

JFK clearly felt a kinship with my father. Both men worked their way across Europe as young-buck journalists. In 1945, JFK got an overseas writing job with the Hearst newspapers, and while still a young senator, he became known as the author of Profiles in Courage. My father made a name for himself in that postwar era as a writer and journalist, and also at a bold young age. In the 1930s, he had biked around Europe, and with virtually no writing experience he talked his way into his first job as a foreign correspondent (in Yugoslavia) for the United Press (UP). After that his talent did the talking, eventually landing him the influential job of European editor of Look Magazine.

The two men found each other because Jack Kennedy was reading and admiring my father's foreign dispatches and journalist's insights. He was especially impressed by an impossible-to-get interview my father had snagged with Soviet Premier Nikita Khrushchev. JFK wanted to bring my father's political chops and youthful energy into his administration. When the president named him ambassador to Ethiopia, Papa was only forty-one years old.

My father never needed training in the smooth pretenses and cool nerves of a diplomat. He was a natural. Hardline-communist Yugoslavia had banned outside currency, so he sneaked his first wages from UP past the checkpoints by hiding his money in cereal boxes. In love—too—he seized the moment with bold confidence. When he saw the woman he wanted to marry, rather than slather her with sticky professions of love, he devised a clever test—also with international implications, to see if she was marriage material. Mummy passed the test, as I will soon explain.

In fact, my mother, Marian Patricia McCarthy (called Pat) was cut from same intrepid stuff as father, though her pedigree was actually finer. While my father came from a good family, he still could qualify as a self-made man. But my mother's blood ran American blue. She is the sixth-generation granddaughter of Benjamin Franklin, and her grandfather, Nathan L. Miller, was governor of New York in the 1920s.

Mummy and Papa met in Europe, where each was pursuing their own high-profile career adventures, which made them excellent partners to—literally—take on the world. The love that my father had for my mother, which was fully reciprocated, was heralded and fierce. The problem was, there wasn't room for more love to give.

❈ ❈ ❈

Given our family track record, it should have been no surprise that at Christmas 2000, we marked the new millennium with a fight. As happens in so many families, the flashpoint was something utterly mundane. I had arrived at my parents' home with a broken nail and asked for some adhesive nail glue to patch it together. This is how a small flame grew into an explosion:

Mummy: "We don't have any glue." (Then she disappeared and came back with a box of forty types of glue.)

Me: "Wow, you have so much glue—wonder which one will work on my nail?"

Mummy (One small beat of silence and then her voice erupted in fury): "You think I have so much? You have no clue what we've being going through and how much we've lost. How dare you say I have so much!"

And so, a small fire flared into a deadly conflagration, with Mummy eventually fleeing to my father's side and railing in a high, harsh voice about what a terrible daughter I was.

I gathered up my things quickly, apologizing as I went. "I'm sorry, Papa, that I can't stay for whatever it is you are cooking for dinner, but I'm obviously not welcome, and I really don't want to ruin your Christmas, or mine. Mummy isn't happy having me here and I've interrupted your writing ..."

Clearly, my surrender was not accepted. An enemy had stormed his castle and upset his Cinderella, and Papa would have none of it. Flailing his wooden spoon in the air, he turned on me full force, and delivered a cruel, final thrust: "You think you're just upsetting her? I don't know why you came. We don't want you here. For that matter, we've never wanted you. We didn't want you when you were born, and we certainly didn't want you when you were a child. We have put up with you as an adult, but we don't enjoy having you around. Yes, I think it's time for you to leave."

"Well, actually, if you notice, I'm saying goodbye," I said, and literally fled into the night.

Didn't want me as a child? Of course, I knew that and always had. I had long accepted what my father thought of me. Years before, I had snapped off all emotional ties to my mother and father, and I gave up trying to understand why they treated me with such dismissive harshness. This much I did know: My father didn't want children at all, and my mother bore children because that's what women of her generation were supposed to do. But actually being a mother? She wasn't interested in that. What she valued was having a career and being a wife.

Early on, I came to understand my mother's self-absorption, and how she treated me had no bearing on my life. I saw her not as mother, but rather, as Papa saw her—as a Cinderella, a beautiful woman who spent her time elsewhere.

Still, my father's bitterness towards me was inexplicable. He could hurl savage insults at me, and two hours later make elegant small talk at a state dinner. He defeated me again and again with cutting barbs, yet he could stagger a stranger with kindness. He treated the man on the street in the same way he treated a president, with deference and attention. But within his family, he lavished his tenderness only on my mother. His love and affection for her was legendary.

****

After that Christmas, I cut my parents from my life completely. So, when my brother Ted called sometime in 2002 to say Papa was dying, the news didn't come as a jolt, but as a small, quiet, tug of sadness.

"I thought I'd let you know in case you want to call him," my brother said. His tone was even and businesslike, as if he was relaying something about a mutual acquaintance. I wasn't surprised, because my relationship with Ted, Kelly, and Alexandra was almost as complicated as my relationship with my parents.

As siblings, we never enjoyed any kind of camaraderie. We had very few common experiences, because we had grown up at different times and even on different continents. By the time I was ten and growing up in Ethiopia, Kelly and Ted had disappeared into overseas schools in England, and Alexandra was still a baby.

So, by the time of Ted's call in 2002, I was already braced to hear unsettling news. Besides, like some people have the gift of spreading cheer wherever they go, my brother and sisters have a gift for doling out uneasiness, and I was often the first in line for a serving.

One especially memorable serving came in a rare email from Alexandra. She confided something to me that I didn't think she or any of my siblings had ever noticed, let alone would have said to Papa on his deathbed: "I hope you say something nice to Deborah before you die, because you haven't been nice to her, her whole life."

Take that, Papa! I knew criticism like that just rolled off my father's back. He truly believed he had done well by us—and in so many ways, he had. Now he was dying, and despite all his past rebuffs, I knew I needed to reach out to him one last time.

I remembered something else Alexandra wrote to me. "You know, Mummy and Papa were the worst to you. I don't understand how you even kept in touch with them."

I told my brother, "I don't think I'll call. I will write him a letter."

Although my heart was breaking a little, I wrote the kind of letter you might send to a second cousin. I told him I was sorry to learn he had cancer, and I'd like to come to see him. A week or so later, he called me to say, "I received your letter, thank you very much, but I'm busy trying to finish my book. Once I finish my book, I'll let you know when it's a convenient time for you to visit."

I wasn't shocked or upset by his response. It was pure Papa. Just as we said good-bye I mouthed into the phone, "Fuck you."

I knew the next time I'd see him he'd be dead—or almost dead.

That moment came in January 2003. My father was in hospice, and this time I didn't wait to ask anybody, I simply flew down to Charlotte to see him. When I arrived at the hospice, my mother was standing guard.

"Can I see him?" I asked.

"No," my mother said.

My brother Ted intervened, saying that—as his daughter—I had every right to see my father, to which mother replied, "Okay, but only for three minutes."

I went in and sat in a chair next to his bed. By then, cancer had stripped away the glossy veneer of strength and health, and his public smile, which was always warm and welcoming. Even so, my father's wasted frame retained something of his authority and presence, though perhaps that was only my imagination willing it so. His career photos of the 50s and 60s—and my childhood memories too—center on a tall, athletic, prematurely balding man, wearing the era's bulky, big-framed glasses—the kind that today might suggest a geek or policy wonk. Back then, Papa's looks radiated intellectual achievement and polish, the looks of a man who never doubted himself. That supreme self-confidence had taken him and our family all over the world.

Now he lay helpless, bloated by steroids and almost unrecognizable. His eyes were closed. I felt the urgency to make these last moments count, but I had no idea how to do it. So, I leaned in close to his shoulder and just began to talk.

"Oh, Papa," I whispered, "I hope you can hear me, because there are so many things I need to say to you. Most of all, I have always loved and admired you! I am sorry you disliked me so much. I do need you to know that I'm okay. I'm happy and my life is good. Thank you for making me the person I am. Because of you I am a strong and self-sufficient person, able to withstand anything, and survive anything, in this world. Ethiopia was the best thing that ever happened to me. It taught me to never feel sorry for myself and to treat everyone the same, to be compassionate and to do for others. I only wish you wanted to know me!"

Then I ended with the one message I knew would make him happy, "I promise to take care of Mummy."

Papa died a week later at home. Now, as I sift through the glitter and rubble of my own life story, the words that come to mind—and which were left unsaid at his deathbed—are these: "Even though you treated me badly, Papa, I did love you so. And I am so grateful to you because oh! What a life you gave me!"

Chapter One

A Driven and Complex Man

Imagine a sixteen-year-old kid, born and raised in New York, who decides to bike through Germany in the late 1930s. This is not the Europe of tea rooms and castle tours, this is the powder-keg Europe of 1938, with the Nazi Third Reich on the march and national borders bristling with tanks and artillery. The boy's parents, who value a good education above everything, can't very well tell him to stay home until he graduates from high school—because he already did that, at age fifteen.

That was my father. He never planned for the future or did the expected, like graduate with the rest of his class. He always had to be pushing ahead to the next new thing, and he always had to be in complete control. Yet, at the same time, he was most happy when he was testing himself against unpredictability and crisis. And for most of his life, he won.

Difficult as our relationship was, I admire my father just as much for what he accomplished as an "unknown" as when he became a public figure. When he was young and feeling his way, he wasn't motivated by material gain or because he wanted to find a comfortable lifestyle—just the opposite. He saw life as a challenge.

If it was up to his parents, winning would have been to see their precocious son become a doctor, like his father. It was classic immigrant dream: get a good education, put in the hard work, and make something of yourself. Papa's grandparents had emigrated in the late 1800s from Eastern Europe, my great-grandfather from Lithuania, and my great-grandmother from Austria. They were determined to assimilate in America and to fit into the mainstream culture, which is probably why I did not know until I was in my 40s that my father's family is Jewish.

My father's dreams for himself were just as ambitious as his parents'—just less obvious. He rejected the bright future of a doctor's life, because he wanted to forge his own way. That didn't just mean testing himself in a career; he also pushed himself as an athlete, and he kept it up even after going overseas. He had been a six-foot-three high school basketball star at Townsend Harris High school in Queens, an academically tough three-year school—and well ahead of its time: the school's president was black, and a lively Friday night for students might be a group discussion on the Russian Revolution.

But even though he was stubborn about following his own path, he showed remarkable patience when it came to at least one of his parents' demands. In retrospect, he recognized it as one of the best things he ever did.

His parents felt their fifteen-year-old high school graduate needed more seasoning, and so they insisted that he put in an extra year at Riverdale Country High School. This was a wealthy and intellectually challenging school in upstate New York.

No question, Riverdale opened the doors for his future life as an ambassador. He always said that the best thing his parents ever did was insist he spend that extra year of high school there. He knew it was a financial sacrifice for them to send him to Riverdale, and he made the most of it.

It was Riverdale that gave him the opportunity to bike through politically-charged Germany in 1938. When he came home, he had an expanded sense of the world, and what he wanted to do with his life.

No wonder he got interested in journalism—and what we today call the media. After graduating from Washington and Lee University with a BA in pre-med, he snagged the most legendary entry-level job in New York, as a page at NBC. Soon the company promoted him to guide at NBC's Rockefeller Center, and for a brief time he even did on-air broadcasting, reading news summaries for NBC radio. But he was restless and quickly took on a second job, writing stories for UP, located about twenty blocks away.

The feisty international news service, which later became UP International (UPI), was outdoing the older and stodgier Associated Press (AP) by pioneering personality-driven stories that featured big name interviews and the writer's byline. In the mid-1930s, UP also became known for its dominance of news coverage in Europe and Asia.

That was enough for my father. UP had bureaus throughout Europe—he could do that! In 1947, UP promoted him to its London bureau. The battered city was still suffering from wartime austerity and rationing, yet it was also rising to the challenges of life after the war. A national celebration was being planned for the wedding of Princess Elizabeth that November, and the city was pulling itself together to host the 1948 Olympics.

But I suspect that my father wanted stories with more meat on the bones. Shortly after he arrived in London, he heard of opening as UP bureau chief in Belgrade, Yugoslavia. The country was in a state of unrest and political transition. Now—that was interesting! Besides, if he was based in Belgrade, that made him head of UP for Eastern Europe, and he would be the only western journalist there.

In fact, two journalists had apparently preceded him, but one had committed suicide and the other had allegedly raped a maid and escaped the country. His predecessors had set a pretty grim record for western journalists, but that didn't deter my father. He marched into the editor's office of UP and said, "I want that job."

His bosses must have been impressed (and probably relieved) that someone was actually motivated to go to that sad country, which was all snarled up in politics and violence. At the end of the First World War, Yugoslavia had been artificially reborn into a monarchy, as a united kingdom of Serbs, Croats, and Slovenes. But by 1948, the king had been deposed and the new Yugoslavia was being run by hardline communists.

Leave it to my complicated, challenge-seeking father—that was the assignment for him.

Only after he won the job did he learn there were strings attached.

First of all, he had to get from London to Belgrade, which stretched some 1,300 miles across the English Channel, through several countries, and over a landscape still pretty torn up by war. So, he was encouraged that UP promised him a car—until he learned the company was deducting the cost of the car from his salary.

Then, to add insult to injury, his bosses told him they couldn't give him any money to live there; he had to smuggle it in. He would be searched at the border, of course, and if he was caught? Well, expect to be immediately arrested for bringing in foreign currency. In effect he was told: "You better figure out a way, Korry, to get it past those guards!"

The helpful heads at UP suggested he roll up his cash and conceal it around his waist, in his belt. (*Oh, of course. They'll never look for it there!*)

My father wasn't at all convinced that was a good plan, and by that time he was getting pretty scared. But fear only kicked his creativity into high gear.

So, here's what he did. He went out and bought boxes and boxes of cereal and chocolate and cigarettes—whatever goods he could find that sounded like reasonable necessities. Then he opened up all the cereal boxes and stuffed wads of cash deep inside, poured cereal over the top to conceal the money, and glued everything back up to look like an ordinary box of cereal. To divert suspicion, he also bought boxes of chocolates and cigarettes, the kind of hard-to-get stuff that would tempt the surliest of guards.

As fortified and ready as he could ever be, he rolled up to the Yugoslav border where he was stopped—as expected—by a phalanx of humorless, gun-toting communist guards. For the next hour and fifteen minutes they methodically ripped apart his whole car, including the back seats. Meanwhile, he played along as the friendly traveler, offering the hardworking guards seemingly endless supplies of candy and cigarettes.

My father, who had the coolest of nerves, said later that was the longest hour and fifteen minutes of his life, with the image of a communist prison cell always before him. He said he would never do anything like that again.

But that is how he got to his job in Belgrade. And despite all the red flags and dangers and discomforts of getting there, Belgrade was one of the best things that ever happened to him.

****

At just about the same time, another New York native, this one from Syracuse, NY, was making an equally gutsy move to build a new life in postwar Europe.

Marian Patricia McCarthy, my mother, finished college in three years and jumped at the chance to take on postwar Europe. The moment came when one of her classmates said, "My father is being appointed as an American diplomat in Hungary and needs a social secretary to go with him." That was all she needed to pack her bags. After settling into her new job, my mother branched out to do some sixty-second broadcasts on radio, which—interestingly enough—also mirrored my father's interests.

After that, my parents couldn't have had less in common, starting with their ancestry. While my father's people were second-generation immigrants from Eastern Europe, my mother's family was one hundred percent American original.

She is the granddaughter (times six) of Benjamin Franklin, and she grew up with the kind of refined privilege you'd expect from the legacy of America's celebrated founding father. To compound the legacy, her maternal grandfather, Nathan Miller, was a prominent New York judge and served as governor of New York in the early 1920s. The only unusual thing about my mother's pedigree was that she wasn't raised in the expected White Anglo-Saxon Protestant model of America's first governing class—but as a Catholic.

Improbably, these two young Americans met in a courtroom in Budapest at the "show trial" of the Catholic Cardinal Josef Mindszenty, who was in the process of being convicted of treason by the Communist People's Court of Hungary.

By that time my father was the UP bureau chief in Belgrade and one of only a few American journalists covering the high-profile trial, which was being followed worldwide.

During a break in the trial, my father saw what he took to be a beautiful Hungarian woman across the courtroom, and his natural confidence told him he had nothing to lose by trying for an introduction. Language was no barrier; both my parents spoke multiple languages, though my father never lost his American accent with a New York tang.

So, he walked up to this woman and said in his best Serbo-Croatian (which was understood everywhere), "It's so nice to meet such a beautiful Hungarian woman!"

To which the woman replied, "What part of New York are you from?

That's how their lifelong love story began. After the trial, my father went back to Belgrade, 200 miles away, and they started to correspond. My mother kept every one of the letters they wrote to each other since 1948.

Even though their bond quickly grew unbreakable, my father wasn't the kind of man who made things easy for the people he loved. I can only imagine how proud he was of himself when he concocted a plan that not only tested my mother's coolness under pressure, but also was designed to help out his new buddies in Belgrade.

His plan came about like this: Papa was a big basketball player, and he answered an ad to coach a local team composed of men from the Union of Metal Workers. The team was filled with eager and athletically impressive Croatians. Even for that era, they were massive men. Some were six-foot-nine, even seven feet tall. Of course, that led to an insurmountable problem: getting basketball shoes that were big enough. Even without postwar rationing, size fifteen to sixteen shoes were impossible to come by in Yugoslavia.

So, here's the challenge he put to the love of his life: "Round up enough size fifteen and size sixteen sneakers, gym shorts, and all the equipment and clothes a basketball team would need—and try to get them past the border checkpoints into communist Yugoslavia."

If she could get through, and not have the goods confiscated or get arrested, he knew she was marriage material.

She did it—and she was.

****

My parents were married on July 7, 1950 in a little Catholic church in Syracuse, NY. But that was the only little thing about the whole event. My mother was never one to hold her light under a bushel, but apparently, she had toned down her family's prominence so much that my father was pretty much dumbfounded when they got off the plane from Europe, and he discovered what kind of a family he was marrying into.

While in most circles he probably could claim the role of a dashing foreign correspondent (bureau chief of UP in Belgrade), in my mother's circle he was still just an up-and-coming news journalist from New York—and an agnostic at that. Meanwhile, her family could claim one of America's founding fathers, a New York governor, and an impressive legacy in Syracuse. To this day, the D.P. McCarthy building is a historic landmark on Salina Street in downtown Syracuse.

Anyway, they were met at the airport by ex-Governor Nathan Miller, my mother's grandfather, who arrived in his limousine bearing the plate-number US1. The ostentatiousness and fanfare would have annoyed Papa a lot, except he was completely charmed by my great-grandfather Nathan, whom he found to be down to earth, interesting, and very bright. After the wedding, they drove out to my great-grandfather's old mansion in Oyster Bay, Long Island, where Mummy had spent many of her summers. I'm sure my father, the journalist and storyteller, was fascinated when he heard what happened to the mansion—after raising his eight daughters there, the former governor sold the family home to the Russian government, which held on to the property until 2016. That year, the diplomats were expelled. It was part of the fallout from the ongoing scandals involving US politicians and Russia. (How Papa would have loved to follow that story!)

Anyway, all the family time and meeting of the in-laws probably went a lot better than my parents expected, but they couldn't wait to get back to Europe. As soon as they could, they booked tickets on the Queen Mary and headed back to Europe for their honeymoon.

If my father felt at all outclassed by my mother's high-achieving family, he was too proud and self-confident to show it. Besides, his own fortunes were about to rise.

After their honeymoon, my parents went back to Belgrade, but it didn't last long. A few months later UP had an opening in Berlin, and Papa took it. He and Mummy lived in a depressing area of the bombed-out city, surrounded by a neighborhood of grey rubble.

By 1950, they were on the move again, this time to a world away from German rubble and hardship. They were living in Paris, and my father, only twenty-eight years old, had been named head of UP for Western Europe.

For a fellow who never planned for the future, my father was doing more than well. His career was on track, he and my mother were happy together, and they were living in Europe—where they both thrived.

At that point, whether by coincidence, design, or accident, they started a family. Of course, to Papa and Mummy, family didn't mean staying home every night, helping with homework, and tucking the kids in bed. My mother was of the generation that believed having children was something you had to do; it was proof of the love you shared with your husband.

Anyway, they had four of us. I was the second daughter and the third child to arrive. Perhaps my parents' most intimate gesture towards me was to officially entrust me with the names of our famous ancestor, Benjamin Franklin, and his wife, Deborah.

And so, Deborah Franklin Korry was born on November 14, 1955 in Paris, "The City of Lights."

CHAPTER TWO

GLOBAL CHILDHOOD

8 Villa Spontini, 16 Arrondissement, Paris, France.

A great part of my soul still lives at that address.

The first house of my childhood was located on a short, gas-lit dead-end private lane of five, late-nineteenth century homes, in a Paris neighborhood known as the 16th Arrondissement. Because I was so very small my memories have no sharp edges; instead, they are dreamlike and magical, mostly about a pretty little garden with the huge overhanging tree—and underneath it—a life-sized doll-house where I played in the shade of summer afternoons.

By the time I arrived in 1955, my sister Kelly and brother Ted (born respectively in 1951 and 1954) had arrived as well. Alexandra was yet to come (in 1959). Our parents were busy with their own lives and with each other, and at least one of them was often away, so our lives were shaped and controlled in many ways by caretakers. The first was Louise, a kindly lady who is just a faint memory to me, though I'm told she faithfully pushed my carriage through the streets that took us past the great Paris landmarks, the Eiffel tower, Arc de Triomphe, the Louvre, and so many more.

Years later, as a young woman in my twenties, I returned to 16 Arrondissement and stood outside our old home, trying as best I could to pull together the sweetest part of my past. Then as now, the old neighborhood was very high-society—very chi chi, and the dignified row of homes resembled a grouping of high-end New York townhouses. It was a neighborhood of rare and unusually large gated homes, too, and bounded by large avenues, famous schools, and lots of museums and parks. On one side of our street stood a small, modern Pasteur laboratory. The area resembled the most fashionable parts of London, Chelsea, and Kensington, where we lived at a later time, when my parents could better afford it.

Our three-bedroom house was built in the English style called Maisonette Anglaise. Its natural, simplified elegance fit my father's influential positions with UP and later, Look magazine—but it did not necessarily fit the family budget. My father's career successes were running ahead of his salary, but piling up wealth was never a prime consideration for him. (It was my mother who needed to live this lifestyle, not my father.)

My parents bought the house by borrowing money from friends and my paternal grandfather, bridging the gap with bank loans. Pricey as it was, 8 Villa Spontini was the right investment. It suited Papa and Mummy (as we always called them), because it became the focus of an exciting world of parties and conversation. In many ways, it resembled the grand tradition of the French salon, where the intellectual and artistic bond together to discuss ideas and the ways of the world while enjoying each other's company. My parents were very social, and my father was away a great deal—but when they were with us, they built an enchanting world of grownup energy and fun.

Tucked in bed, we children strained to hear the magical world that was springing to life in the rest of the house as another cocktail party got underway. As the house filled up with guests, we were lulled to sleep by the comforting and exotic scents of the ladies' lovely French perfumes mingling with the pungent smoke of Gauloise cigarettes, and the sounds of laughter and rapid-fire conversations in English and French.

I spoke French before I spoke English, but soon was moving easily between both, which is probably why—to this day—I feel very comfortable meeting people in large groups and chatting with strangers. To be able to speak fluently in more than one language has given me throughout my life a confidence, and an intangible easiness with foreigners—no matter where they are from, even if I don't know their language.

Certainly, as a child, meeting people from all over the world forced me to stay on my toes. I have faint memories of skittering through the house during a cocktail party, on my way back to my bed, and bumping into the legs of grownups as tall as trees, who would sometimes bend down and ruffle my hair. These were invariably kind and clever people who asked me kindly what my name was or challenged me with a question, such as whether I had learned anything interesting that day. So, I knew very early on what it was like to be around grownups. I liked to listen to the rhythm of these parties and was often lulled to sleep by the steady thrum of people talking and laughing in a nearby room. The women's voices glittered like silver and mingled with the deeper currents of the men's voices, which rumbled like distant trains passing by. These were "Papa and Mummy's friends", and only later did I appreciate that they were famous too.

One of these friends was the future senator, Daniel Patrick Moynihan, who was larger than life even then. Later on, Senator Moynihan and my father would share destinies as ambassadors in the Kennedy administration. They also shared a love for life overseas, and especially for life in Paris and London. Our family memories include Pat Moynihan and his brother sweeping Mummy off to dance the night away in one of Paris's many jazz cellars, which was a special craze in the 1950s. The future senator would become known for his intellect and public policy stands, but he also had a playful and irrepressible side—and a wonderfully boyish, Irish mischievousness. My mother tells how, at the end of one particularly exuberant jazz party, he somehow managed to do a handstand in the car as they sped down the Champs-Élysées in the early dawn.

My father considered these lively personalities to be not only his friends but professional sources and colleagues. My mother, on the other hand, was completely happy as a social being. She was temperamentally suited to be a socialite. She wore her beauty easily, and the fact she was also very smart made her all the more attractive to the quick witted and educated circle they cultivated. What's more, her pedigree as a direct descendant of the incomparable Benjamin Franklin made her a unique celebrity in her own right, and a ful crum for many witty jokes and clever teasing about her illustrious ancestor. After all, Franklin's crowded resume included the fact that he also knew Paris well, as America's first ambassador to France.

In so many ways, my father and mother were perfectly suited to the life of the salon. These were people—including my father—who shaped the ideas and public policy of mid-century America.

One of those people was Priscilla Buckley, the sister of William F. Buckley, who lived in Paris during that time and became my parents' lifelong friend. Like my father, in the 1940s, Priscilla worked for UP in New York, then returned in the 1950s to work in Paris with my father. She wrote a book about being an American journalist overseas called String of Pearls, a title that captured the elegance required of reporters in that era, even in the hard-bitten gumshoe world of news reporting. Later, Priscilla would become managing editor of her brother's National Review, the magazine that shaped and inspired conservative thought in America for generations.

But my parents' friends ranged across the political spectrum and included people of many interests. One was a fellow UP alumnus Marquis Childs, an unabashed liberal who won the Pulitzer Prize for commentary; another was New York Times reporter Richard Witkin, who also worked in Paris at the time and became known in the 1960s for his historic coverage of America's early manned space flights. He and my father were close friends until my father's death.

But not every friend had to have a "name." Papa enjoyed visiting a bistro called Monteuil in Les Halles, the famous working-class district of Paris, which was also a favorite restaurant haunt for writers and intellectuals.

In the 1970s, when visiting Paris with my brother Ted, my father wanted to stroll down to the old bistro.

The former owner was long gone, but Papa had questions for the new proprietor. "Anyone left from the old days?" he asked.

"Do you remember Pierre?" the bistro owner asked, to which my father exclaimed, "The busboy?"

"Yes! He has his own bistro now." That was all Papa had to hear—he took off down the street toward the shop owned by Pierre. They were barely inside the door when Pierre looked up and beamed—after twenty-five years, he knew my father right away. From that one meeting, they remained friends for the rest of Papa's life, and my parents even visited Pierre and his family in the country home where they retired.

To Papa, it didn't matter whether the individual was a former busboy or from a patrician family like the Buckleys—he saw every adult as interesting and worthy of attention. But children were a different story; children needed to get some age on them, like a good wine. He said later that children were not interesting until they had reached the age of reason (the age when a child can first distinguish right from wrong). According to my father, that high bar wasn't reached until the teenage years.

Of course, Papa's philosophy (which Mummy shared) affected me and my three siblings. It meant that our childhood in Paris and London was spent mostly in the company of nannies and coping with long stretches of silence while my parents were happy, busy, or away. I have faint and melancholy memories of my mother driving him to the airport to catch a plane for the continent, or for New York, or hearing my father roar off to the office in the family Renault or the economical Simca.

Throughout my childhood, my father always seemed to be going away.

While my father was gathering news, my mother was gathering friends and interesting job opportunities, all of which—both friends and jobs—were attracted to her like moths to flame. While in Paris, she became social secretary to the second-in-command at the American Embassy and also volunteered for the American Rescue Committee at the time of the Hungarian Revolution.

She was very creative and versatile. One day, when a fashion editor failed to appear at the last minute for the Paris spring openings, my father, who by then was European editor of Look, quickly recruited my mother to fill in. What Mummy lacked in experience she made up for in her natural style. In fact, she did such a good job at that spring opening that she ended up with a regular reporting assignment covering the famed fashion houses of Dior and Balenciaga and other great names of Paris fashion.

It was an unbelievably exciting time to be in Paris for this revival. In less than a decade after war's ravages and enemy occupation, France was already leading the world again in style and setting the standard of haute couture. Despite having no experience in the language of fashion—or with the tough competitive women who covered it—my mother knew how to hold her own.

As for Papa, his path to Look came about partly because, by the mid-1950s, he was getting restless. He was idealistic and a dreamer, which meant he was always looking for the next big thing to capture his imagination. He wasn't ambitious in the ordinary sense— he never thought about the financial end of things or planned for the future—but he was ambitious about how he could challenge himself next. He was most interested in what was going on in the world and being at the center of historical events. He wanted to make a positive contribution and educate people. Everything else had to fit into that mindset, and even though he loved her dearly, that included his wife.

His idealism and sense of rightness didn't necessarily fit in the lockstep world of corporate journalism, which apparently was where he felt UP was drifting. He didn't like the fact they wanted to edit his stories by altering the facts. My father had the rock-ribbed conviction that journalism is about reporting events and ideas objectively, and it is for the individuals who read the information to interpret as they wish.

So, in 1955, he left UP—and in a rather dramatic way that became legendary. He wrote a story which the editors wanted to substantially change, which was a complete affront to Papa's commitment to objective reporting. So, he simply up and quit—even though he was only a tantalizing six months away from collecting a full UP pension.

That was my father. Yes, he was willful and self-confident to the point of being self-absorbed, but he also had a commitment to the truth of things. Anyway, maybe he was prescient about the future of UP, because a few years later it merged with the Hearst outfit, International News Service, to become UPI. Inevitably, the culture there changed even more, and in ways he probably would have liked even less.

By that time though, the dreamer and idealist had landed squarely on his feet. He was hired by Look magazine to lead its operations in Europe. Not only was Look a wonderful place to work, it would set the stage for a surprising twist in Papa's future.

Look magazine had been launched in 1937 by Gardner (Mike) Cowles, editor of the Des Moines Register and Des Moines Tribune. He was a son of Gardner Cowles, head of the legendary newspaper publishing family. Mike wanted to create a magazine to meet "the tremendous unfilled demand for extraordinary news and feature pictures." Right away, it started a friendly rivalry with Life magazine, Henry Luce's publication which had launched a year earlier. Look pioneered bold, stylized imagery and short, punchy phrasing, which set it apart from the wordier approach of Life, which was a sister publication of Luce's Time. But in that era, when American publications could do no wrong, both picture magazines easily co-existed.

It was rather tragi-comic, the way my father first forged his ties with Look. In that big-family way journalists have of bonding together, he already knew Mike Cowles, because Cowles used to work at UP. So, when Cowles and his wife, Fleur, decided to head across the pond for a vacation, it was natural to look up my parents, who had already become friends. Given the time frame, I suspect that Papa and Mike Cowles were also planning to explore the prospect of my father joining Look.

Anyway, it was 1955 (Mummy was seven months pregnant with

me), when my parents went to the Paris airport to greet Gardner and Fleur as they emerged from their first-class cabin.

In those days, you could wait for passengers on the tarmac as they came down the stair ramp. As the Cowles' walked across the tarmac, Papa stepped forward to greet his future boss, while Mummy headed toward Fleur.

But instead of seeing the bright, fixed smile of an approaching guest, my mother was horrified to see that the elegant blonde coming towards her was absolutely shattered, her face distorted by tears. "Whatever is the matter?" my mother gasped, thinking her guest was ill or they had received an emergency overseas cable about a family death.

Between sobs, Fleur Cowles managed to say, "He has just asked me for a divorce."

From that moment on, the whole visit took on a surreal note. My mother, who was not easily rattled, was completely thrown off her game and stammered out the first comforting thing she could think of: "Would you like to be the godmother of my child?"

Fleur, just as rattled, burst out "Yes!" and that is how this lovely, legendary figure became my godmother. (This is my mother's story, and obviously I was not a position at the time to verify it, but it must be substantially true because my godmother and I did establish a relationship of sorts later on.)

The Cowles divorce happened, and afterwards my godmother Fleur married a successful English architect (good for her!) and that marriage (her fourth and last) took her already exciting career to another level.

In the early 1950s, Fleur Cowles had already become a style celebrity in her own right, first as founder and publisher of a fresh and influential fashion magazine called Flair. (To give an idea of her range, after she died in 2009 at age 101, Christie's was commissioned to auction off her enormous collection of paintings, furniture, clothing, and objets d'art. The auction house identified her as "the legendary editor and society figure ... a renowned journalist, author, artist, patron, and fashionista ...")

That was only the beginning of the descriptive accolades. Fleur Cowles was so talented, in so many different ways, that the national media found it hard to turn off the faucet of words to describe her. She was widely quoted as saying, "I have an idea a minute. I'm a born idea myself."

And so, this "Friend of the Elite" (that was only one of the descriptions in The New York Times obituary) became my godmother.

She may also have had more of a say in my father's future than anyone knew at the time. According to The Times obituary, after she married Mike Cowles in 1946, she let her husband know she was ashamed of the downscale look of Look—she said it had a "man's barbershop" quality to it. She urged him to make it more stylish and sophisticated, and goaded him to move the headquarters from Iowa to New York, where she was born.

So, that meeting with my parents in 1955 may have been not just a vacation, but an excuse to evaluate my father for the position of European editor of Look. Plus, it's not hard to believe that Fleur Cowles would have been seriously impressed with my mother's patrician background—and she may have figured an editor with such an aristocratic wife must have the kind of panache her husband's barbershop magazine sorely needed. As for Fleur herself, she apparently had to manufacture her own high-end background from scratch (according to The Times obit, she was born with the name Florence and rose from "modest beginnings").

If that was true, well, that was Fleur. She created her own life as a work of art. But as far as she and I were concerned, godmother status never led to any particularly magical connection between us. She was more like a shimmering presence in the background of my life. She created a few paintings for me, which were lovely, and once I remember visiting her in England when I was about twelve and thinking, "Oh, I wish I could just stay here and live with her forever!" I loved her apartment, I loved all her paintings and artwork and all her many, many beautiful things—and most important of all, I loved her because she was nice to me.

But mostly, Fleur touched me from afar, through her hauntingly beautiful artworks featuring animals and nature, which The Times praised in her obituary this way: "Her paintings of jungle beasts, huge flowers, birds and objects of nature, often in dreamlike sequences, were exhibited in cities around the world."

Years before, when our family was actually living in an exotic locale of exquisite flowers and animals, I would think of my godmother many times and her fabulous art—and the bond we shared because of our mutual love for animals and nature.

****

However, I barely had time (literally) to absorb all these wonderful things Paris had to offer, because when I was three years old, everything changed. My father's position as European editor of Look moved from Paris to London. By then my sister Kelly, brother Ted, and I were chattering effortlessly in French and had been successfully weaned on La Marseillaise, the Tricolor, and Bastille Day.

Then, all of a sudden, we were plunged into the land of Churchill, shepherd's pie, and the Union Jack.

Gone was our beautiful Maisonette Anglais, the nearby Bois de Bolougne, and its beautiful lake. In its place, we moved into an eighteenth-century house on St. Leonard's Terrace, right across the street from London's historic Chelsea Royal Hospital and stately gardens. At the time, the hospital was nearly 300 years old, and a gem of English architecture designed by the incomparable Christopher Wren. We stayed there for several months, until my clever mother finished converting two dilapidated, side-by side, nineteenth century flats in southwest London into a beautiful home known as 4 Ennismore Gardens. Our new home was just a quick walk, in three different directions, to Hyde Park, the Victoria and Albert Museum, and Harrod's.

At Ennismore Gardens, we had a couple who cooked and cleaned for us: Mario and Anna, who were from a small town in Sicily. They taught me my first Italian words, "Bella Bambina! (Beautiful child)" which, to my delight, they bellowed at me at every opportunity.

Then Nursie arrived. She joined us in November 1958, a few months before my sister Alexandra was born. Nursie's real name was Emily Stanbury, and she had the cachet of having been the nanny to a young New York couple, Cy and Marina Sulzberger. Cy was son of Arthur Ochs Sulzberger, the owner of The New York Times. (Even our nanny had ties with the scions of American journalism.)

Nursie stayed with our family for eighteen years, through several countries, and many family crises. Thanks to Nursie, I learned discipline, manners, and the joy of keeping a diary. Nursie taught me to knit, sew, and learn my timetables (a very British skill). Through Nursie I learned hand crafts, like building my own dollhouse and creating my own thank-you cards. Nursie taught us that when you came home from school, you didn't run around or hang out, you went to your room and worked on a project.

Nursie was a real English governess, tough and unbending. At the time, I couldn't stand being told to: "Sit up straight!" "Wash your hands!" "Hang up your jacket!" Nursie's rules were enough to make one's head ache. But, later in life, I realized all the skills I learned from Nursie have served me very well: I have great posture, I'm very organized, and I can practice good manners even on auto-pilot, if I have to.

Although Nursie cared for all of us, Alexandra was born on her watch, and they formed the closest thing to a real mother-daughter bond, which lasted until Nursie's death. As for me, I felt I had to fit into Nursie's system as best I could, and because I was the third in line (and my two older siblings were already growing independent and living away), I often felt singled out for punishment.

Certainly, Alexandra had most of Nursie's affection. One of the few reminiscences Nursie told about me was a rather grim little story involving rain. We had been in England for about a year, which meant I was about four years old. One day, Nursie was hurrying me along through London streets to catch a bus, and—as usual—the streets were shiny with a grey drizzle that never, ever seemed to end—though that day there seemed to be an odd pause in the dampness.

I was sulky and unhappy, and as we boarded the bus, according to Nursie, I looked up at the sky and said, "I don't like that up there! What is it?"

"It's the sun!" Nursie exclaimed. It was her favorite story about me.

Meanwhile, my father was attracting a following. During the time he was European editor of Look magazine, from 1954 to 1960, his reporting earned him the Overseas Press Club Award for maga-zine reporting and a Page One Award from the American News-paper Guild. In this period, he wrote extensively about liberation movements in Africa, and he had arranged for his boss to interview

Soviet Chairman Nikita S. Khrushchev, something no journalist had been able to do.

It was the Khruschhev interview that got John Kennedy's attention. JFK and my father shared a number of things in common—they had both achieved great success by their early 40s, and largely in the same way: through writing, journalism, and politics. When John F. Kennedy took office as president of the United States in January 1961, one of the people he was interested in bringing into his administration was my father—and you can kind of imagine JFK saying it, "Let's see if we can get that guy at Look, Ed Korry!"

One cold grey day in London, my father picked up the phone, and it was a transatlantic call from the office of the president of the United States. In subsequent conversations, many assignments were considered—was my father interested in speechwriting? Something in the press secretary's office? Writing policy papers? What was he interested in?

Most of all, Kennedy (at age forty-three, the youngest person ever elected president) wanted an administration marked by youth and vigor. He wanted government to be led by the people of his generation—the first generation of leaders to be born in the twentieth century. He was intrigued by my father, who was five years younger than Kennedy, and who had already proven himself by his heavy-duty reporting from Communist Yugoslavia and two of the most important capitals of Europe.

My father was a tough New Yorker too, so Kennedy knew he could take a bruising in Washington. And I'm sure it didn't hurt that Ed Korry's wife came from a prominent Catholic family, just like the Kennedys, and she had an even better bloodline that stretched straight back to Benjamin Franklin—a founder and architect of the country. I'm sure that historic twist intrigued JFK enormously; it was one of those unique, dramatic details that had to tug at the writer and journalist in him.

Plus, Ed Korry was head of Look magazine in Europe, one of the most prestigious jobs in publishing. ("Let's try to get this guy over here!")

But my father wasn't interested in coming to Washington.

This is one of the things I admired about Papa; he was always his own man. He was never interested in power, and while he was fascinated by politics, he wasn't interested in being in politics. He saw through a lot of that and considered it hollow ambition and ladder-climbing. It was the thrill of getting the story, being a participant on the world stage, that captured his interest. Years later, if you asked him to give an example of a successful moment in his life, he wouldn't immediately pick out being named to a powerful position—no, he would say it was getting that interview with Khrushchev. That was the kind of achievement Papa cherished.

Anyway, that's how he caught Jack Kennedy's attention—by getting that Khrushchev interview. The new president needed background and advice on how to approach and understand Eastern Europe. Today, the Cold War is regarded as something of a historic footnote, which is a serious misreading of the danger of the times. In the 1960s, the whole world recognized the Cold War as a serious threat, maybe a threat to global existence itself. In that world, my father had judgment and experience.

So, my father became a presidential advisor to Kennedy on Eastern Europe. He began commuting from London, where he still worked for Look, and met regularly with JFK and the administration officials in Washington and New York. But gradually, he began to take on a number of extra projects, both in and out of government. He attended the Harvard Advanced Management Training program, for example, and eventually moved us to New York, where he did special projects for Look magazine.

In a spicy sort of twist, during this time one of his extra projects in the Kennedy administration was to sit on a panel to review potential candidates for ambassadorships. A few months later, Kennedy turned the tables on him—by asking my father to become an ambassador himself.

We had been living in New York for about eighteen months when Papa became the ambassador-designate for Ethiopia. By then I was six or seven years old: big enough to understand this was a big deal. Next thing we knew, we were on our way to see the president at the White House where Papa was going to be sworn in.

My father—sworn in! The whole idea consumed my imagination: a plane trip across the ocean, a new dress, a tour of the White House, and then to be in the Oval Office with President Kennedy—how grand!

A photo was taken of all of us on that momentous day. There's me, looking pensive in a sweet, ruffled-collar dress, white socks, and little black mary janes. My mother is dressed in a proper Chanel-style checkered suit, the kind of outfit First Lady Jacqueline Kennedy had made popular. President Kennedy is saying something in midsentence, and it's clearly something charming and funny that has made Papa—six-foot-three, trim, smiling, and confident—break into a grin. My three siblings, Kelly, Ted, and Alexandra are there too, and so is our grandmother—who surely was thinking that her daughter had not done badly in the marriage department after all.

I remember the president's daughter, Caroline (she was about my age), running in and out of the Oval Office that day, and I remember looking at her kind of wistfully—the way a lonely child does, because I wished we had time to play together.

Then all of a sudden President Kennedy was bending down and

taking off his tie clip and putting it on my brother Ted, who was all dressed up in a proper suit and tie.

That was a fitting end to an unforgettable day, and my memory of it would have been entirely sweet, I think, except for one little incident afterwards.

As soon as we left the White House, my father reached down and yanked off the clip that President Kennedy had fastened on my brother's tie. It startled Ted, and I remember the look of hurt that flashed across his face and I thought, "How could Papa do that?" It was the worst thing—when we had all been so happy. Papa kept the clip for many years until, I suppose, he felt Ted was old enough to appreciate and treasure it (and not let it fumble out of his ten-year-old hands and into a storm drain). In retrospect, Papa probably did the right thing, but the way he did it caused a wound.

But Papa quickly gave us other things to think about. He always wanted to test our knowledge and curiosity about the world, so he posed this question: "President Kennedy has offered me a job, and it's going to be in another country—a country that begins with "E". What country do you think it is?"

In our family, by age five we were expected to know things, like the countries of the world, so when Papa asked the question, he was not being playful. He expected us to come up with an answer.

"England!" Of course, it had to be England! (Except it wasn't.)

"El Salvador?"

"Egypt?"

We never guessed the right country—not right then—yet for me, that country would help define my life. Not only that, it would teach me what it means to have a country to love.

CHAPTER THREE

A COUNTRY THAT BEGINS WITH "E"

Our plane glided through the clouds into Addis Ababa, the capital city of Ethiopia, in March 1963. Rainy season was sweeping in, and we couldn't see much of the airport below, because it was overcast. But the clouds did nothing to flatten my excitement.

Papa had promised us "a country that begins with E." He loved piquing our childhood curiosity, and we had responded: England? Ecuador? El Salvador? Egypt? We threw back every answer we could think of—and still hadn't guessed it.

When Papa finally told us the name, I—for one—was thrilled. Ethiopia! It sounded exotic and beautiful to the ear, and there was a mad rush to find it on the desk globe—where, exactly, was Ethiopia? On a brand-new continent we had never visited before, Africa! And this was not just Africa, but the Horn of Africa. To really live there—in the sub-Sahara—sounded impossibly adventurous and daring.

But the wonder hit all of us in different ways. My older sister, Kelly, wasn't invested in this adventure at all—she was living with friends of my parents in New York while she finished school. My brother Ted was with us for only about six months, then he was going off to boarding school in England. That left me and Alexandra, and she was so small, she was content to be anywhere as long as she had Nursie close by.

My father spent the hours on the plane reviewing papers. He was all business. He was immersed in world politics, had already served on important advisory panels, like the Council on Foreign Relations, and had taken on other national global and assignments. My father knew the importance of Ethiopia in regional and world politics, and so he took the weight of his new ambassadorship with great seriousness. My mother, characteristically, was determined to shine—wherever she was. In Paris, London, or New York, she moved in a world that suited her. What would she find in Ethiopia?

As for me, by age seven I had already lived on two continents, in three countries, and visited many others. The world already seemed a great adventure to me. I knew hard truth that comes to a child who is used to a certain amount of loneliness and forced on her own devices. In other words, I was already resourceful, inquisitive, and ready for the next big thing.

Well, maybe not quite ready. As our plane glided onto the runway, we were startled to see a huge crowd come into view. Wait a minute—they were there for us! A band struck up music including America's "Star Spangled Banner" and other high-spirited tunes. The American ambassador had arrived.

Staff from the American embassy, both Ethiopian and American, were there to greet the new boss, and so were dignitaries from the office of the Emperor Haile Selassie (whom we would meet later). Ethiopia was striving to be a forward-looking nation. It had been aligned with the United States since 1903 and played an increasingly pivotal role in world politics during the Cold War. Emperor Selassie had governed since the 1930s, and his goal was to be allied with modern times and, most of all, with America. With Soviet pressure growing throughout Africa, Ethiopia was a stabilizing influence in the sub-Sahara region.

That's why, in a very real way, the weight of the world was on my father's shoulders. President Kennedy wanted to continue strong relations with Ethiopia. He made it one of the first countries to take part in his new Peace Corps program, and it grew into the largest Peace Corps program in the world. In October 1963, JFK would invite the Emperor Selassie to Washington for a state visit, a posh affair also attended by my father.

So far, our arrival on the tarmac that day, the flurry of flowers, the music, the friendly welcome, all pointed to a good beginning. I made sure to look closely at the faces in the crowd, because Papa had taught us to be curious about everything. His favorite saying was, "Curiosity is the mind's best index to freshness." He believed that to stop being curious was to stop learning. From childhood that lesson was steeped into my bones, and so by the time we arrived in Ethiopia, I was eager to learn everything.

Many ethnic strains flow through the people of Ethiopia, and while this was a country much more exotic than I had ever known, I was never afraid. In fact, this was my first sight of so many people who did not look like me—and I was thrilled. Even though I was a child, I somehow understood that Ethiopia was not just one thing, but many complex things, and it had many gifts to give me—which would stay with me for a lifetime.

There was a little welcoming ceremony. Papa said a few words, and then we were nudged into a long, black limousine, which glided like a long, black shark through the capital city. We learned that, before heading for our new home at the American Embassy, we were being taken for a special tour of one of Ethiopia's crowning achievements.

On the way, I peered out of the window into a brand-new world. Addis Ababa sits in a plateau of the sub-Sahara, surrounded by the

Entoto mountains. Unlike the green leafiness of the parks and boulevards of Paris and London, my first impression of Addis was the
tans and browns and sharp shadows of a desert landscape, giving it
a haunting beauty I couldn't wait to explore. In the 1960s, the city
was in the making: a jumble of things, both modern and decrepit.
Boxy, modern-like buildings, monuments, and shabby shops co-
existed on the main streets, but there was an energy too, because
under Haile Salassie, a great period of modernization was underway. Newly planted eucalyptus trees lined the main streets, and a
main gathering place, called Meskel Square, was alive with people.

As we glided by in the long limousine, we passed women carrying big baskets balanced gracefully on their heads and children
running along in ragged, rumpled clothes, without shoes. Other
people were dressed in traditional Ethiopian clothes made of a woven cotton cloth called (as I learned much later) shemma; others
were in western dress, just as you would find in any urban city in
the world. As I learned later, when world leaders came to Ethiopia—and that included ambassadors—those kinds of well-dressed
urban people seemed to magically multiply, and the city was all
spruced up. For example, when Addis Ababa hosted the visits of
French president Charles de Gaulle and Britain's Queen Elizabeth,
the city went through a complete transformation of scrubbing and
cleaning. Roads were fixed, and every poor person—it seemed—
had a pair of shoes.

When our limousine reached the outskirts of Addis, everything
changed. We were now passing through the areas dominated by
tukuls, which are Ethiopian mud homes with thatched roofs. The
streets were unpaved, the sidewalks nonexistent, and the people
I saw had that helpless and trapped look of people who have no
hope. Even as a child I could see that. I saw children my own age

wearing scraps of rags, with flies swarming over their dulled eyes, absolutely bereft of the joy of play and laughter.

It was too much to absorb all at once, which was okay, because all of a sudden, we had arrived at our destination. As a sign of welcome, the Ethiopian officials had promised to show Papa and his family one of the government's crowning achievements—a leper colony.

(A leper colony! I loved animals! What an exciting way to begin our life in Ethiopia—we were visiting a new kind of animal I had never seen, an animal that was part of my new country!)

I don't know what my parents thought at that moment; in a rush the doors of the limousine were opened for us, and we all piled out to walk around the leper colony. At first, the colony looked exactly like the neighborhoods of poverty we had just driven through: mud huts and poor people everywhere. The officials invited us to simply walk around, and one of the escorts politely pointed the lepers out to us: ("See how well we take care of them.")

I was only a child, but in one confused and sickening rush I suddenly understood what a leper was—a real human being, just like me, but a human being whose limbs were all torn up and mutilated by a horrible disease called leprosy.

Why, why did they have to look like this? Does this happen to everyone in Ethiopia? Were the beautiful and handsome people at the airport just there for show? I felt as if we had been tricked. But even more, I was struck with compassion and empathy, though at the time I didn't know those words. I wanted to run up and hug every one of those people with the strange name: lepers. I wanted to take them with us, to do something, I wanted us to help fix them.

The grownups held me back, they didn't want me to go near them. Back in the limousine we went, as if this disturbing visit had never happened.

It turns out the Ethiopians have no prejudice against leprosy—in fact, they are proud of the humane way they care for them. The contagious ones live in a leper colony, and visitors—like us—are safely welcomed from afar. Lepers also walk freely in the streets, and they are treated as naturally as we would treat someone who is walking down the street with a cane.

As we piled back in the limousine, I remember how the adults were all chattering away. (Maybe from nerves?) As for me, I was very quiet. My emotions were difficult to sort out, but I remember feeling sad, perturbed, and helpless. The lepers had opened my eyes to an unexpectedly tragic world. Through new eyes, I saw that the streets were filled with beggars, people without limbs, and row after row of mud houses—real poverty. Poverty I had never seen before. I felt guilty, sitting in a beautiful car being chauffeured around. I wanted to crouch down on the car floor and hide. I couldn't bear to think that one of these poor people might be able to look into the car and see how fat and pampered we were.

But then we pulled up to our new home, and Ethiopia showed us another one of her faces.

The American Embassy compound was in a world of its own. Big gates set it apart from the world outside, which was street after street of poor housing. But inside the gates? The Embassy grounds were impeccable. Green grass, beautiful trees, flowers … it looked a little like Hyde Park in London, where Nursie would take us children for afternoon walks. Except these grounds were more businesslike, the trees were sparse, and there were no shady groves or smooth lakes where we could play. As our limousine rolled up the boulevard, we saw an American flag flying.

"There's the White House!" I said. The building in front of me looked as magnificent as the home of the handsome American president with the kind eyes, who had stooped over to shake my hand, and who had given my brother his very own tie clip.

But that's not to say I felt in any way American. My time in the USA had been far too short. Naturally and instinctively, I was a child of Europe and Britain. Now, I was eager to learn how to be a child of Ethiopia.

****

One thing the compound didn't have was a school. Every day, I hopped into the big black limousine to go to what we called the English school.

I had come to hate that limousine, because it set me apart from everybody. But I loved our limousine driver—his name was Fanta, and he was among first of many characters and unforgettable friends I made in Ethiopia.

In the early 60s, Fanta was the name of one of the soft drink brands sold overseas by the Coca Cola Company. Along with Coke and Sprite, Fanta was a big deal in Ethiopia.

"Do you like being called Fanta?" I loved challenging my new friend with the question, which I did over and over again, because he was so nice to me and always played along. Fanta would always grin back at me and say, "I came before the drink!" Because of Fanta, even though I despised the limousine, I always looked forward to the ride to school, except I did everything possible to crouch down so no one on the street would see me. I was ashamed to be driven around in that shiny monstrosity that set me apart from everyone.

One day I was in the limousine with my father—one of the few times we rode together—and suddenly he pointed out the window and said, "Deborah, don't ever think you're better than anyone else. You're no better than that beggar on the street, or the person who cooks your meal, or who serves you food. You may be sitting in this car right now, and we may be living in a big house, but it's all temporary. Never forget—I don't own any of it."

I was only seven or eight years old, but I never forgot my father's words. The curious thing was (and I often pondered it later) my father never practiced empathy himself, at least not toward me—but he knew very well what it was.

No, it was Ethiopia, not my father, that gave me the gift of empathy. Now, when I'm in New York, waiting in a restaurant for a friend, I try not to get annoyed wondering, "Why is she late?" Or if someone can't find a certain brand of bread or a shade of lipstick, or they can't get tickets to a concert, or reservations at a restaurant at the time or on the night they want, I think: "God, if people only saw what people in other parts of the world go through, just to be normal, to have one cup of water!"

****

The streets of Addis Ababa showed many levels of poverty, while the English school represented a more prosperous cross section of the world. Classes were taught primarily in English, though there was an emphasis on French and on learning Amharic, the official language of Ethiopia. Amharic is a Semitic language, with a script that looks Hebraic or Arabic. For a westerner, it's not easy to learn, which is why I am grateful for the opportunity to do so as a child. The enrollment was about 380 students. Most of them were Ethiopian, though diplomats from other African countries also sent their children there, because it was a good school. There were Israeli children and some Italian kids too. Prior to World War II, Mussolini had invaded Ethiopia, and after the war some Italians stayed and created their own Italian-Ethiopian community. However, my class was mostly Ethiopian, except for two Israelis, one Italian, and one other American. Though I was in the minority, so to speak, I never felt out of place. The Ethiopian children became my friends. I never saw color.

Thanks to Ethiopia, I grew up truly color blind. This was another gift from Ethiopia, and it had lifelong implications which I came to understand only years later when I was an adult living in the United States. Wherever I was: a grocery store, cocktail party, or a beauty salon—if I saw an African-American (or any black person from any part of the world, not just Africa) and we caught each other's eye, we would spontaneously say hello. How could this be? We were strangers. We had never met. But it happened over and over again. There was some natural affinity that was unexplainable. I was curious about it and one day asked an African American acquaintance why she thought it was happening.

"Do I remind you of anything as an African American?" I asked. "What is it that I have, that practically every African American smiles and says hello to me?"

"Deborah," she replied, "it's not just every African American. If you notice, everybody says 'hello' to you. You smile when you see people, so they just smile at you. And you make eye contact. Very few people do that—especially white people!"

That's when I realized it was the Ethiopian culture which had made me more open and natural to everyone I met. Surface appearance meant much less there, especially when it came to ethnic differences. I'd grown up with mostly brown and black-colored people, so color had no bearing on me. We all grew up together.

****

One night, I woke up crying. By the time Nursie had rushed in,

I was half awake and her stern voice broke through my sleepiness. "You've had a nightmare," she said, as if she was ordering me to believe it. My heart was thumping away. In the darkness, I almost had to go over, again and again, what made me weep.

My nightmare involved one of my new school friends, Elena, a little Italian girl. We weren't close for long. She was older and a little self-important, but she took it upon herself to take me around and introduce me to everyone else. I remember her gratefully, because (thanks to her) I soon had many friends.

But that night, I dreamed Elena died while eating pizza with her family. It was terrifying—the idea of my friend: being so happy, eating a pizza, and then dying!

Two months after my dream, Elena and her family got on a plane to visit Italy. It was her first trip to the country of her ancestors. But they never arrived. The plane crashed, killing everyone aboard.

Nursie was alarmed. She saw my dream as evidence of a strangely gifted, but disturbed, child. She interpreted the pizza in my dream as a symbol of Italy, with Elena's death following close behind.

Nursie reported all this to my parents. "There must be something wrong with Deborah," she said. "She is too intuitive, or she has a sixth sense. This is not healthy behavior in a child."

Nursie was haunted by that incident. Some twenty years later, she still reminded me of that odd coincidence of my nightmare that foretold Elena's death. It was not the last time I had an eerie premonition, or some kind of inner message, about something that would happen later in real life. And it's true, other odd and disturbing things happened in Ethiopia, which followed me into my later years.

But here is yet another gift from Ethiopia: every single thing that happened to me in that beautiful, memorable country made me stronger and braver. They gave me the determination to take on life boldly.

****

But I didn't need nightmares to make my heart thump in the night. Over and over again, I would lie in bed and listen to weird he-he-he sounds and maniacal laughter coming through the dark. As I looked at the shadows floating across the curtains in my bedroom, I imagined these shadows were actually the weird cackling creatures dancing closer and closer to me ... now they were right outside my window! My skin prickled as I imagined that soon they would be inside, joining me in a dance across my bedroom.

Hyenas: those were the demonic-sounding creatures whose images danced across my curtains! Hyenas are a fact of life in Addis Ababa. They live in the foothills outside the city, and they even prowl the city itself. At dusk, as the white noise of daytime fell away, I would hear a series of hair-raising sounds like no other animal sounds on earth. They can mimic the human-like laughter of an ax murderer in a frenzy, then slide into a series of weird groans and grunts, followed by high pitched wails and insane-sounding giggles. Despite the fact that hyenas are fearsome predators, with a bite more powerful than a great white shark, Ethiopians have coexisted with them for centuries—even in cities. But that doesn't mean they aren't regarded with healthy fear and caution and given wide berth. In the city, we would often catch a glimpse of one hyena or (far more unsettling), a pack of them trotting down a road with their strange, gimpy gait. With their ravenous faces and sloping backs, they looked like mutated dogs or animal-demons, waiting to pounce.

From an early age I loved animals, and so the hyenas fascinated me (though love was a stretch.) My love for other animals came easily, especially when it came to three special ones—Ajax, Napoleon, and Florence. These were among my first friends in Ethiopia. My two older siblings were away, my parents were absorbed in their own lives, and (at an early age) I came to understand that I would have to build my own life too.

So began my lifelong love affair with dogs. Ajax (which we pronounced in the German way, as A-yax) was the first. He was a German shepherd that had been given to us by a Polish family that was going home after a diplomatic tour in Addis Ababa. Napoleon and Florence were rabbits I found scampering on the compound grounds. I cared for these little creatures like a mother caring for her young. I was a solitary child who woke up every day with purpose and hope, because I had my animals to care for.

Then one day, I suffered my first family loss—Napoleon was missing from his cage. I panicked and created such a fuss that the United States Marines assigned to the Embassy left their guard and fanned out across the enormous grounds to look for my pet rabbit!

Hours later, one of the Marines came to me with sad news: They had found the tattered remains of my "child", Napoleon. Even worse, the killer was my beloved Ajax. It took me a long time to forgive him, but I was learning to be tough. I needed friends, and so eventually Ajax won my heart back.

I had horses too. Ethiopians love horses, and it's said they are more popular than bicycles (at least they were then), because horses were easier to come by than bicycles. The previous U.S. ambassador, Arthur L. Richards, had built a horse stable on the grounds. With it came the groom, named Sa'id, who became another of my new friends. Sa'id had worked for General Nils Palmstierna, who was part of a large group of Swedish advisors in Ethiopia, but Sa'id wasn't happy in his job. My father offered him the groom's job, and Sa'id became a trusted member of the Korrys' extended family. He made the adjustments to the stable, and soon I was spending much of my free time learning how to groom a horse and how to ride. I remember three horses with great wistfulness and affection: Ghana was our show horse and had a dramatic, circus-like stride; Maroon was a fast racing horse with a long mane, and Whiskey was a beautiful, dove-gray horse with a luxurious mane and a sweet personality that, in many ways, made me love her the best.

****

There was also a raw and brutal side to Ethiopian life. It didn't spring from viciousness—Ethiopians gentle and kind—but because, like many under-developed countries, the people have learned to live with a depth of deprivation, hardship, and pain in ways we have banned from our western laws and culture.

I faced this right away in school. In biology class, for example, if we were discussing an animal's anatomy, it wasn't uncommon to have an animal slaughtered right there in the schoolyard. Then we would be instructed to pull the intestines out, stretch them out right there across the playground, and measure them.

I hated biology. But far, far worse was to come. It had to do with the quick, permanent punishment that was standard operating procedure in Haile Selassie's government.

In short, virtually anyone who committed the smallest of crimes was hanged. Thieves and adulterers were hanged. Apple snatchers were hanged just as quickly as traitors were hanged. It seemed like the tiniest wrongdoing led to hanging.

And hard as it may be to believe, our schoolyard was used for some of those hangings. We had a beautiful, big schoolyard, so it was easy to put up gallows and take them down again.

I was seven years old when I saw my first hanging.

The school principals announced we were all to gather in the schoolyard, as if we were going to a special event. We walked outside, and a huge crowd was there, including all the teachers, as well as government officials. A weeping woman and two children were standing there too. Then a man, clearly one of their family, was led out to the center of the field where a wooden platform had been set up. He managed a few sad goodbye looks to his family, and then soldiers quickly and efficiently put his head in a noose slung over a makeshift gallows. And then he was hanged.

I wasn't sure at first what I was seeing. In my head a buzzing began (I suppose it was shock), and then I was aware the Ethiopians standing in the crowd had begun a mournful chant in their native Amharic language. A real, living human being had walked out on our playground, and now he was just a limp body, swaying in the sunshine. I was in the audience of a horror movie that had come to life.

This was my first hanging. Over the next few years in Ethiopia, I would witness many more.

My little sister, Alexandra, was in a pre-school in another building, and she had been spared these sights until one day, when we were leaving school together. I was responsible for collecting her at the end of each day, and as usual she was holding my hand. Suddenly a huge crowd of students surged around us, and we were in the middle of it, propelled helplessly back into the schoolyard. I tried to shield Alexandra but couldn't. She was only about four, and terrified. When we got home, she ran shrieking to Nursie: "Deborah just showed me a hanging!"

Right away, Nursie spanked me hard and promised the worst was yet to come. That night, Alexandra woke up crying and screaming.

That was enough for Nursie—she told my parents, and my punishment was very painful: Papa and Mummy stopped speaking to me for a whole year. Whenever they were near me, they acted as if I didn't exist, and when we were all in a room they addressed everyone but me.

People find this hard to believe, but maybe it makes sense if you understand that my parents believed I was an incorrigible child, spoiled and willful, who had deliberately subjected my little sister to a traumatic event. Maybe they were advised—by Nursie and others—that I would learn to behave if left to my own devices. Then they became busy and went off into their own world. After all, they knew I was being taken care of. Or maybe they just forgot about me until I grew up.

Anyway, I never spoke to anyone about the hangings again; they became literally unspeakable. But here is the strange thing: hangings have followed me throughout my life. A roommate at my boarding school in New York hung herself in our room. Later, in Chile, a family maid was found hanging in a closet of our home.

Did that trauma I experienced as a child in Ethiopia touch off some horrible energy that has followed me into later life?

Was Nursie right? Was there something strange and disturbing about me that attracted death and tragedy? Surely that wasn't possible! But it was a darkness that stalked me just the same.

****

Because I was a solitary and resourceful child, I found a refuge from the things that troubled me, which mostly sprang from my relationship with my family and Nursie.

A series of caves buttressed the back of our compound, and I was drawn there. Late at night, after everyone had gone to bed, I would sneak down the corridor and follow the escape route I had plotted out during the day. (In the early 1960s, government security was easy to deconstruct, even for a child.) A few turns through the darkened halls, a few doors opened, and I was out on the lawn, sprinting through the shadows toward the caves. They were cool and quiet, a salve from the hurt, and a getaway from too many people. An embassy compound is always bristling with people. The caves became my refuge, especially after my parents began to shun me. The caves were my own special secret—a place I could dream freely and think about a future where I would be in charge of making my own happiness.

One night, I fell asleep there. About four hours later, I'm startled awake by Nursie's voice way in the distance, calling my name.

Now I was in for it. Nursie had notified my parents, who had notified the US Marines assigned to the Embassy, and everyone was out looking for me.

I remember being sorry the hyenas didn't find me first. My parents never physically abused me, but the fury of their tongue lashings crushed and bloodied me even more (or so I imagined) than a hyena's jaws that were stronger than a shark's.

And so, I became a survivor. I learned then not to count on anybody except myself, and I resolved to succeed in life all on my own. That quality of self-reliance was something I learned young. So were the qualities of empathy, color blindness, boldness, and the ability to recognize grace and beauty, even in modest and impoverished things. These gifts, and many more, were given to me by Ethiopia.

CHAPTER FOUR

THE EMPEROR NEXT DOOR

When I first saw him, I thought he was a kid, all dressed up.

I had built up in my mind what a grand and mighty emperor this Haile Selassie must be. Before we were presented to him as a family, my father, wearing a top hat and black formal wear, had been summoned to the palace to present his credentials as the new United States Ambassador to Ethiopia.

When it was our family's turn, I was shocked to realize that the emperor of Ethiopia was shorter than I was and may have weighed even less.

I remember being coached to present myself with a curtsy (a ritual I always detested) and to address the emperor as Your Majesty. For our first meeting, he was wearing a long white cape over a white tunic; I wore a high-colored white dress with a big sash. I remember when he took my hand, his hand was soft and fragile. Yet, his eyes were keen and intelligent, and when he smiled, my child's instinct told me he was kind, he liked children (he had six children himself), and he respected me.

Selassie may have been a tiny man, but he had a very long lineage. He was regarded as a direct descendant of King Solomon and the Queen of Sheba, who reigned some 3,000 years ago. Selassies' ancestry followed the Rastafarian religion, which regarded him as the Messiah, but he himself was an Orthodox Christian. He was tolerant and supportive of both Ethiopia's strong and historic Christian presence and the country's Rastafarian history.

To celebrate his lineage and power (and undoubtedly to remind the populace who was boss), Selassie kept a menagerie of live lions on the palace grounds; in fact, when you pulled up to the palace compound, one of the first sights was a pair of live lions, sitting on each side of the palace gates. Inside, portraits of lions hung on his palace walls. His full title, which was rolled out for state occasions and events, read like this: "By the Conquering Lion of the Tribe of Judah, His Imperial Majesty Haile Selassie, I, King of Kings of Ethiopia, Elect of God."

While he did not look it, this diminutive man with the tight, drawn face and sad eyes was a major leader in mid-twentieth century global politics. By the time President Kennedy dispatched my father to Ethiopia in the early 1960s, Selassie had been the country's ruler for thirty years. He had led his people through war, Italian occupation, and exile. Through many political and personal challenges, he remained a visionary who wanted to make Ethiopia a great country. He abolished slavery, encouraged modern architecture, and was a leader in founding the Organization of African Unity (OAU), which valued a strong friendship with the West. Selassie had many enemies in the Marxist-leaning African states, so he was ruthless in keeping society in line (as noted by the nearly daily hangings), and he was shrewd in picking his friends. Among his best were the Americans, French, and British.

He must have enjoyed the arrival of Anglophiles like my parents. After Mussolini invaded Ethiopia in the mid-1930s, Selassie was exiled to Britain, where he lived during the first years of the Second World War. I can only imagine the many interesting conversations that he had with my father about their shared affection for life among the British. In fact, when Britain suffered a massive flood in 1947, one of the countries which responded quickly with emergency aid was Haile Selassie's Ethiopia.

But the Lion of Judah had a many-sided personality, as we would find out. For example, (who knew) he was also a fellow who enjoyed a good dinner and a night at the movies.

Until my father became ambassador, the American embassy in Ethiopia was not exactly a citadel for lavish entertaining. Other embassies considered it part of their diplomatic duty to show off America's glamor and goodwill in a big way—but not in Ethiopia. In fact, an invitation to an evening at the American embassy on Entoto Street was politely considered to be a forced duty, where guests endured dull food and stiff hospitality for the sake of diplomacy.

Then my mother arrived.

Suddenly the American embassy was the place to be. This was what my mother was made for—creating glamor, wherever she went. Singlehandedly she elevated the dinner party and events of state to a work of art. She understood that Ethiopians didn't want to be invited to the American embassy to eat Ethiopian food—they could do that at home! They wanted to eat the way the Americans and the French did. She also recognized a basic but powerful human emotion—all other things being equal, on a night out, most people want to have fun.

It didn't take long for this new diplomatic strategy to filter over to the palace. After that, there was no suave wrangling for an invitation. Emperor Selassie's people simply called up the embassy on a Thursday to announce, "We will be there Monday night for dinner."

"We" to Emperor Selassie meant an entourage of 100 people, including his whole family and his children, plus staff and security people.

Well, what of it? Entertaining a crowd on short notice didn't faze Mummy—she just went to work. It strained the limits of the nearby PX (which was run by the US military), but within forty-eight hours' notice she always managed to deliver a menu that celebrated the best of western cuisine. She especially stressed the French gourmet experience, which was prized all over the world. Top-flight American food, like beef shipped in from Kansas, was also considered an exotic treat. Even American peanut butter was considered by the Ethiopians to be a strange, but delectable, delicacy. And to embassy guests, even that American staple, the sandwich, was considered an exotic hors d'oevre.

My mother didn't just envision the menu—she was, in effect, the head chef as well. She commandeered the kitchen staff and trained her sous chefs, and then created a beautiful menu card for each guest, which was placed at each dinner setting.

One menu I have saved and cherish was a celebration of exquisite Gallic pride: The dinner opened with consomme de volaille (a clear soup), followed by quenelles de brochet (a delicate fish in a cream sauce), capped with a hearty filet de boeuf roti (an expertly done beef roast). Each course was polished off with the magical addition of a fine Montrachet ('62), Le Chambertin ('61), and Moet et Chandon ('59). These finest-of-the-fine French wines appeared seemingly out of nowhere—definitely not out of the PX—thanks to an Ethiopian with connections.

If my mother had been a movie producer, her mantel would have been lined end-to-end with Academy Awards. When it came to entertaining and serving up the finest of food, she was that good.

But the evening wasn't over yet. What mid-twentieth century party thrown by American hosts would be complete without a movie? After dinner, everyone regrouped into the large foyer that

THE AMBASSADOR'S DAUGHTER • 59

was transformed into a movie theater with folding chairs and a big screen.

Emperor Selassie didn't speak English comfortably, so my father would hitch his folding chair next to the emperor's knee and translate the movie dialogue into French (which goes to show there are no end to the skills needed by a good ambassador.) I'm sure Papa also drew on his skills from his journalism days, when he had to listen to, and then summarize, multiple radio news stories simultaneously.

My favorite image and memory of movie night at the embassy was seeing my father pulled up close to the emperor to translate the high-jinks dialogue of Father Goose, a movie starring Cary Grant and Leslie Caron, set in the South Seas. It was one of Selassie's favorite films.

No doubt about it, the emperor had a soft side, despite looking so rigid and stern in his photos. For instance, he was a dog lover whose most special companion was a little chihuahua named Lulu. The story has it that he always traveled with Lulu, who would sit politely in his lap, at least most of the time. But if there was a reception, Lulu would be let loose to circulate around the room and scamper between the legs of the guests. It was said that this resulted in important reconnaissance work for the emperor, because the rumor was that if Lulu sensed someone didn't like Haile Selassie, she would touch the man's foot, which was a signal to the emperor not to trust that man.

By then, I was growing into a precocious child who noticed everything, and when I saw this tiny little dog in the arms of this powerful man who ruled with a fist of tempered iron, I remember thinking, "Gosh, this is so weird! Here's this big important guy with lions on his wall, and he carries around this tiny little dog. My dog, Ajax, is nine times this little dog!"

I realized this was one of many interesting mysteries about human beings. Ever since, I've paid attention to people who are dog owners and tried to figure out the connection between the size and type of their dogs and what it says about them as an individual. As for the emperor, perhaps one clue into his love of dogs was the fact that, since his youth, Selassie had been surrounded by political intrigues at the palace, and probably felt he could trust no one completely—except his animal friends.

The story of Lulu had a sad ending. Years after we left Ethiopia, we learned that one of Haile Selassie's big palace dogs had grabbed Lulu by the neck and shook her until she was dead.

Haile Selassie may have been the Lion of Judah, but knowing what I did of this complex man, I'm sure the loss of Lulu left him close to heartbroken.

****

The protocol of Ethiopia made life interesting, if rather stringent. Even for the American ambassador and his family, invitations to palace events weren't really invitations; they were veiled orders to be there. Yes, Ambassador Korry and his family represented the most powerful nation on earth, but Papa could never say, "Well, I'm sorry; I'm busy tonight. I can't make it."

Even more complicated was the possibility of driving somewhere and having our car cross paths with Emperor Selassie's vehicle. If that happened, there was only one thing to do—get out of our car and bow to the emperor! This was an awesome and majestic gesture of respect, but it led to some funny moments for us, especially when we were trying to sneak away for some private getaway time.

One favorite getaway was an afternoon picnic. It was a chance for Papa to slip out of his ambassador's role and into a pair of shorts.

My mother and Nursie were in the car of course, and sometimes visitors and friends, who sometimes included high-ranking American or Israeli military officers. But it didn't matter who was with us—if we got word that the emperor's car was approaching, Fanta had to pull over to the side of the road, and all of us had to get out and be ready to bow.

Meanwhile, Papa was positioning himself to the left of the side door, hoping the emperor would not call him over for a conversation, and thus expose his diplomatically shocking pair of knees.

Another protocol ritual was the curtsy, which I especially hated. Every time we went to a palace event, I had to curtsy. When people came to our house, I had to curtsy. I couldn't stand it. Even as a child, the ritual of paying deference to another human being in such a robotic way felt false and offensive.

These elitist rituals—forced invitations, curtsying, bowing at the side of the road—made a lasting impression on me. How could one group of people behave as if they were better than other people?

Yet, I also was learning the varieties of world culture, which was immensely valuable in understanding human beings. In fact, through the years I became so empathetic to the Ethiopian culture that (unconsciously) I have even altered my accent to reflect my love of that country. For example, I have often spoken English with an Ethiopian accent, even when speaking to other Americans. "Why are you doing that?" my companions will gasp, and I think, My ear has been so well trained to listen and think like Ethiopians that sometimes it feels like the normal way to express myself. I also think that growing up in so many cultures—English, French, Ethiopian, and Chilean—has given me an unconscious kind of empathy, so that I tend to adapt my own speech to the language or accent I am listening to.

Clearly, Emperor Selassie knew the value of being able to move easily among cultures. One of the ways he reinforced this skill was by making sure we children at the English school were getting a well-rounded education.

I remember one day, he came to the English school and embarrassed me immensely. We were at work on our lessons when it was announced the emperor had arrived for a visit. He wanted to make sure all children were studying Amharic—and learning Ethiopia's native language well.

And who better than the American ambassador's daughter to spring a quiz on? I was called up to the front of the class, which I resented. I was one of six foreign students in class (no sense testing the Ethiopian kids on their own language), and the emperor wasted no time putting me through my paces.

"Are you learning the language well?" he asked me, in Amharic. I replied as best I could. He wanted to know if I was able to speak Amharic with my friends, what new words I had learned that week, and so on.

How annoyed I was! Without notice, I was forced to carry on a conversation with the emperor of Ethiopia in front of my teacher and the whole class, and I felt I wasn't well prepared. But thinking back, I was already bilingual and spoke French before I spoke English, and the guest of honor seemed satisfied, so I think my instinctive language skills probably carried me that day. Now, I look back on that quiz with great affection.

As trying as the event was, I felt that day, as I always have about Haile Selassie, that he had a warm and welcoming spirit. He was not autocratic by any means, and I was never afraid of him, nor in awe of him either. To me, he was a small, thin man with a warm smile that—like his eyes—seemed to carry some sadness within.

****

In October 1963, a great excitement was building up. Papa was accompanying Haile Selassie to America for a state visit. I remember it was a very big event, because this visit would showcase my father's critical work in Ethiopia, and the huge role Haile Selassie played on the world stage. It was also a historic moment, the meeting of the African leader and the president of the United States. And it was a serious visit too, because Marxist forces were increasing their political pressure throughout Africa, including in Ethiopia. In 1963, Selassie led the effort to found the Organization of African Unity (OAU), which the West (and the White House) hoped would be a stabilizing influence in the region. A great deal was resting on my father's shoulders.

The visit was a success, but for me, there was something even more pressing that loomed in my life: my eighth birthday was on November 14. I was especially excited because Mummy and Papa had promised that, on the following weekend, I could celebrate with my first ever birthday party.

Usually Nursie came in to wake us up, but on the day of my party, Mummy walked in. I only had to take one sleepy look to know she wasn't there to say, "Happy birthday." She was dressed all in black and looked as if she had been crying.

In a flat voice she made an announcement: Papa's boss, President John F. Kennedy, had been killed, and my birthday party was canceled. Then she walked out.

The news was still fresh, at least for those pre-internet days, and it reached the American embassies in lightning time. But because of the time difference the date was one day later than history records it in America, and it happened to coincide with my birthday party, scheduled for November 23, 1963. At first, I just lay there in bed, trying to process it all. I would like to say that my first emotion was to be completely devastated by the tragedy. But no, I was ticked off because my first real birthday party had to be cancelled.

After Mummy left, Nursie came in and got us dressed with military precision. In a sorrowful but brisk English way, she filled us in about what was known so far, but it all boiled down to one terrible thing: Papa's boss, John Kennedy, had been assassinated.

Little by little, as the details sank in, I began to think less about my birthday and more about the handsome president who gave my brother a tie clip, whose eyes crinkled when he laughed, and who told our family funny stories, so we would look happy when the photographer snapped pictures of us in the Oval Office.

Nursie didn't give us time to grieve, even though she let us know that she felt terrible that my birthday party was canceled, and that we children had to be involved in the tragedy at all. However, she told us that we had to buck up and act like a family that represented President Kennedy and the United States of America. She said that people would be coming to the residence all day long to pay their respects, and we had to be dressed and behave properly. It's hard to process in our age of lightning-fast communication, but in 1963 for ordinary people around the world, the news was coming in slowly, and they expected us to know.

I remember people filing into our reception room, weeping— Ethiopian, French, and British people. Staff from other embassies came to pay their respects to America, and to offer personal words of sympathy for the Kennedy family, as well as for my parents and us children, just as if the Kennedys' were our blood relatives. At this time of grief, Ambassador Korry and his family were America's family.

Emperor Haile Selassie called for a day of national mourning in honor of America's Catholic president; the Catholic church in Addis Ababa held a funeral mass. Then, Haile Selassie, accompanied by my father, returned to Washington for the funeral in the city they had visited so successfully just a few weeks before.

****

When my father returned again to Addis Ababa, he was drained and devastated. He and Jack Kennedy had shared a natural affinity, and he regarded JFK's death as a personal, as well as professional, tragedy.

I remember Papa sitting at a table in our dining room where a large group of trusted guests and friends had gathered to hear about his experiences in Washington and at the funeral. Papa was still devastated and still bitter about the callous transfer of power that he perceived over just a few days. He talked about how shockingly offensive it was to hear "Hail to the Chief" played during the funeral procession. The tune is meant to celebrate a living president, and the message it conveyed was that leadership had passed to a new man, Lyndon Johnson. But the funeral was meant to be for mourning, not to celebrate new leadership.

Papa was even more upset when he went to the Oval Office to meet President Johnson before returning to Ethiopia. JFK had been dead barely five days, and Papa said there wasn't a single artifact or remembrance in the office to evoke that John Kennedy had ever governed there. Not a picture, not an ashtray, nothing. In less than a week, all the vitality, energy and purpose that JFK had brought to the presidency—and to history—had been wiped out of the Oval Office.

Papa's bitterness about the way Kennedy's presence was banished

so soon after his death has stayed with me all these years. Sometimes I think, "Why do I remember that so clearly?" and I realize
it's because it shows so clearly how fleeting life is and how quickly
anyone can be replaced—including me.

Another devastating change came about ten years after the death
of John Kennedy, and this change was also personal to us.

After more than forty years on the throne, Emperor Selassie's
rule was overthrown by a Marxist government, and a massacre
followed.

Emperor Selassie was imprisoned, and his friends—all our
friends—the entire middle class and educated people of Ethiopia
were hunted down, tortured, and imprisoned. Many were executed.
These were people who came to our dinners and had us into their
homes. They taught in my school; they were my classmates and
friends.

Fanta, our chauffeur, was likely spared because he had left Addis Ababa long before then; Sa'id, who managed our horse stable,
was saved because, mercifully, he died of diabetes before the government net tightened.

Haile Selassie was kept under house arrest in his own palace, but
essentially, he disappeared from view. The official news came in
1974 that he had died of "natural causes," but a strong undercurrent
of rumors suggested he had been brutally executed.

It was heartbreaking to think about his last days—he was a cul-
tured man, gentle and powerful. Despite the weight of his ancestry and everything that went with being an emperor, he had very
endearing human qualities. He loved American movies and good
conversation, he was kind to kids, and he cherished animals, especially his little chihauhua. Yes, he also used oppressive means to
keep his country in line, but his goal was to keep order and stability,

which was very different from the wholesale roundup and slaughter of innocent people devised by the Marxist forces that finally overcame him.

My father often spoke of Haile Selassie with great respect and admiration, and he felt a deep sadness at the brutal ending of his life. Papa saw Selassie as a true visionary whose goal was to make Ethiopia the crown jewel of Africa, as well as a model of civilization and education. He was a man who led his country into the League of Nations and promoted African unity, who was a friend to the United States and to the Kennedy administration. Selassie was refined and educated, a man who spoke several languages and could move in different cultures. Papa also admired him as a man of decisiveness, who showed great physical and moral courage when necessary.

However, this was interesting: While my father developed an admiration and affection for Selassie, the emperor showed no true affection for my father. My father was just one of many foreigners he had been dealing with over the years. In fact, when my father went to say goodbye, Selassie offered no gesture of affection at all, no gratitude for Papa's years of service, no acknowledgement—even for the sociable evenings at the embassy and those movie nights when Papa translated dialogue at his knee! No, his attitude was one of complete indifference.

Part of his coldness could be traced to hard political realities. My father had resisted many of Haile Selassie's demands—most notably to supply more US arms to the Ethiopian government. In turn, Selassie had resisted my father's advice to make the country truly modern, and therefore resistant to Marxist influences. There are many Ethiopians and US scholars who have written that had Haile Selassie listened to my father, the bloody overthrow of Selassie and his government wouldn't have taken place.

For me as a child, Haile Selassie was my first real image of a leader. It wasn't the American president or the British prime minister who earned my awe and shaped my childhood memories; it was a slight and fragile-looking Ethiopian man who loomed large over every day of my early life. I'm sure my love for Ethiopia was greatly shaped by his presence.

He and I especially shared a love of animals, and maybe a distrust of our fellow human beings, too. There is a quote attributed to Haile Selassie that fits this complex man, and certainly fits the tragic end of his life. The Lion of Judah was sadly prescient when he said, "It is much easier to show compassion to animals. They are never wicked."

CHAPTER FIVE

"ETHIOPIA WILL ALWAYS BE WITH ME"

When my father returned from Washington in December 1963, after attending John Kennedy's funeral, everything felt unsettled and grim, even though on the surface things seemed to continue as before. Lyndon Johnson had called my father into the "new" Oval Office, swept clean of Kennedy's presence, and told him he wanted Papa to stay on in Ethiopia. But of course, no one knew how long that would be.

Nobody asked me, but I was eight years old, and I'd already fallen in love with Ethiopia. The thought of being taken away was intolerable. I devised defiant getaway plans in my head, like leaping on one of our horses, Whiskey, and galloping into the hills with a trove of food. My idea was to convince Sa'id to drop me off somewhere in the network of caves, so no one could ever find me.

I loved Ethiopia that much, and I love it to this day. What I learned there shaped me as a person, and it will always be with me. Yet, living in Ethiopia I also learned how contradictory life is, that nothing in this fleeting life stays the same, and there is very little that can be trusted to last forever.

Funny, though, the one change I feared during that tragic year—to be taken away from Ethiopia—didn't happen. Instead, other changes were rushing in like an invisible riptide—in Papa's career, in political pressures in Ethiopia, and in me.

On Christmas Day, 1963, I was eight years old by one month, when I experienced something strange. We were sitting around the Christmas tree, opening our presents. I remember I was in a white dress, sitting in my usual tomboyish way, when my sister Kelly bolted to my side and said in a panicky voice:

"Quick! Get to the bathroom," she said. "You're bleeding!"

I was too confused to be scared. I had no idea what was happening, and Kelly didn't explain further, except to push me forward into the nearest bathroom, where she shoved some thick white pads in my hands and told me how to position them inside my panties. Then she delivered the most confusing information of all—this would happen to me every single month.

And that was my Christmas Day 1963. I cleaned myself up, and we went back to the holiday festivities. The day went on the same as before, but I remember feeling disconnected from things. I was bothered by the noise of all the Korrys talking over each other (hardly a new phenomenon) and besides, I had a terrible stomachache and an odd sensation of cramps, which I had never felt before. Plus, I think I was in a little state of shock, trying to figure out what this bloody attack on my body was all about. But strangest of all was the fact that Kelly, who was almost five years older than I, went right back to the festivities without a thought about what I had just experienced.

On one hand, this incident may prove Mummy wasn't exactly pro-active when it came to teaching her daughters the mysteries of womanhood. On the other hand, she was of a generation that stayed silent about these mysteries until a daughter reached the requisite age of thirteen—and after all, I was only eight!

Much later—long after I had figured out things for myself—I learned that in Ethiopia, most girls begin to get their periods at about age eight. This is far different than in westernized countries, where the average age to begin menstruation is eleven to thirteen. It's been documented—and even given a name: menstrual synchrony—to describe the phenomenon that females who cluster together (on sports teams, in dormitories, and in small communities) tend to menstruate at the same time. In a related way, the average onset of menstruation follows different patterns in different parts of the world.

Looking back, this seemed to me one more proof—maybe the most dramatic proof of all—that Ethiopia, this country I loved so much, had truly made me one of its own, even in the secret depths of my own body.

****

No, I never wanted to leave Ethiopia, and for nearly five years, until October 1967, I was able to live in the hope that I never would. The new president, Lyndon Johnson, wanted Papa to stay on as ambassador. He trusted Papa's expertise in African affairs and asked my father to write a report on what US policy should be in Africa for the next decade. My father's analysis, which became known as the "Korry Report", was issued in 1966. It recommended that US aid be concentrated in the African countries that emphasize development, and that the World Bank be enlisted to provide external aid for the rest of the continent. This strategy was adopted, and President Johnson clearly valued Papa's advice and counsel, because he would go on to offer him three very good positions in the administration. However, as I shall explain, nothing about serving a president of the United States is ever straightforward.

For me, living in Ethiopia was never straightforward either. Just like my childhood and womanhood came together in such an intense and startling way, in Ethiopia, many contradictory things co-existed together for many years. All of them worked together somehow to make me the person I have turned out to be.

One of my most enduring memories was picking one of my horses from the stable and galloping into the hills outside of Addis with Sa'id, ducking and weaving through the stands of thorn trees that looked like the fingers of gnarled old women who had once been beautiful.

The landscape we explored near Addis—a city which stands at 9,000 feet, nearly two miles above sea level—was harsh and brown and looked unforgiving. But I loved it, probably because the landscape reflected my private world as a solitary child, forging my own path over challenging emotional terrain. I never felt scared on these rides and found it exciting to think that hyenas roamed these hills, and at any moment we might encounter gazelles, wolves, horned ibex, monkeys, and even elephants.

Beyond the brown hills, if you rode far enough, were sunny plateaus and mountains and green pastures that appeared like magic, where lions roamed free as well—what a wonderful thing if we could encounter them too! When I was with Sa'id, every adventure seemed possible. I was a loner and let very few people into my life, but I loved and trusted Sa'id. I felt safe and comfortable escaping into the hills with him at my side. Sa'id represented freedom to me. He became my friend, teacher, and bodyguard.

So, I wanted to explore everywhere and try everything. I was growing into a self-reliant and somewhat cocky young woman, and it was important to me to test my self-confidence.

One day, I dared Sa'id to take me to the mountain caves to find a man who was the subject of strange rumors floating around Addis Ababa. This man was supposedly an American who had become strangely fascinated with hyenas. He went out into the country of caves to find the hyenas and disappeared. It was said he was living in the caves with the hyenas and howling along with them, like one of their own.

But Sa'id, who was not afraid of anything, was afraid of that. "No, no, Debritu," he said (that was my name among the Ethiopians), "I will not go anywhere near that man. It is very dangerous ..."

It was true. An element of danger always seemed to flow like an undercurrent under Ethiopia's beauty. I experienced this firsthand myself. We had a special high point place we called Korry Mountain where we would occasionally treat ourselves to a picnic lunch of American and French food (and Nursie's inevitable watercress sandwiches), while overlooking the far-below city of Addis Ababa. I remember that our picnics—despite being well over 9,000 feet high—could never escape the flies. It was always a contest between us and the flies. There were so many of these whirling flecks of torment all around us that it became funny—my father would brag about how many he'd killed.

While the adults picnicked and swatted flies, we kids would swarm around the mountain, which is where I experienced one of my first real personal crises: I suddenly felt something sharp, stuck in my eye. All of a sudden, I was seeing approximately half what I did before. I walked back to the picnic site, but the adults, chatting away in picnic-talk, hardly noticed us. I was expected to be tough and strong and not complain, so I said nothing.

Later, I confessed to my mother, and she fashioned a patch over my eye, until the aching torment of light and blurred vision became so obviously abnormal and alarming that Mummy finally arranged a flight on a small army plane to see an eye doctor at the American military base in Asmara.

It turned out that during my hike up the wind-blown side of

Korry Mountain, a microscopic piece of metal had flown into my eye and wedged itself across my pupil. The doctor in Asmara used a magnetic tool to remove it. He promised me if I wore a patch for a month, my vision would come back.

As an athletic kid, a tomboy who knew no fear, broken or sprained arms were nothing new for me, and they produced nothing like the terror of thinking I had possibly lost the sight in my left eye forever.

In an odd postscript to the story, many years later a fortune teller revealed, with dramatic effect, that she "saw" I had nearly lost my eyesight when I was young, and that I was fortunate to have finally been taken to an eye specialist before I had permanent damage to my eye.

****

Maybe the experience of losing sight in my eye made me more curious about the terrors and fears other people experience. Even though I was growing to be a very self-contained person who didn't want to get too close to anyone, on the other hand, I was curious about all sorts of people. I was always unafraid to approach strangers and invite them to speak with me. Because I could get by in Amharic (and French was a familiar language in Ethiopia), I was confident about talking to people on the street, whomever they were—old men with missing limbs resting in the shade against a building; young women, carrying food, quiet and dignified in their beautiful white veils; or children begging for affection—I wanted to meet everyone. Inside of myself, I stayed private and inaccessible, yet that didn't stop me from wanting to know everything about these strangers, what they were thinking and doing and wanting.

I especially loved playing with Ethiopian children. I felt an affinity with them. I related to them, whereas I didn't relate to the

American children who stayed aloof in my experience and seemed to think they were better than the Ethiopians. I would grab food off my lunch or dinner plate in the Embassy, wrap it in one of the white linen napkins, and sneak it out of the house to give to the Ethiopian kids who played with me in the compound. Nursie loved feeding us the one-note tastes of British food, marmite and watercress with butter sandwiches, but the Ethiopians, who love spice and strong tastes, didn't care much for those English staples. But what they did love was American peanut butter! I l loved watching their faces light up as they bit into the gooey, thick stickiness of peanut butter on bread; it was another shared experience that made us good friends.

In turn, I joined them in their soccer games on the embassy grounds, and they taught me new things, like how to make finger rings out of eucalyptus leaves. To this day, I remember the names of these friends: Abel, Mariam, Anan, Genet, Tesfaye, Samsen, Ashenafi, Sumeya, and Ahmed ... I loved them.

I felt like a true Ethiopian when we ventured into the crowded streets for the great yearly festivals of Addis Ababa, which has been a center of religious faith for centuries. Ethiopia was one of the earliest outposts of Christianity, and during the mid-twentieth century they still celebrated with colorful festivals such as Timkut, which draws thousands to the public streets. Timkut revelers celebrate the baptism of Jesus by putting on snow-white tunics and red sashes, and carrying scarlet umbrellas covered in velvet and gilt braiding. At Meskel in September, which celebrates the finding of Christ's true cross and the end of the rainy season, bonfires blazed up in the middle of large Meskel Square and the streets are lined with yellow daisies, which are a symbol of Ethiopia—after the rainy season, they bloom over the Ethiopian landscape like a beautiful explosion.

In fact, the name Addis Ababa means "new flower." Rastafarian practices are also celebrated in Ethiopia, including the belief that Haile Selassie was the Messiah, although Selassie himself was an Orthodox Christian. The emperor didn't discourage the Rastafarian beliefs in his unique role, which is another example of the many complexities woven into the Ethiopian culture.

It turned out the Ethiopians were curious about American festivals too. When we arrived in the spring of 1963, it became known that everyone was expecting the American ambassador to throw a real celebration on the Fourth of July. Not that Americans were seen as party experts—in fact, based on past experience, most Ethiopians weren't impressed by American celebrations or cuisine, but they were curious just the same.

Well, Mummy didn't need to hear more—they wondered how Americans threw a party? No sooner said than done!

I vividly remember the huge tent that was pitched outside our embassy home, and the buzz and excitement about that big billowing canvas set that slowly raised off the ground as the Fourth of July approached.

Then Mummy upped the ante. She had a passion for jazz and could sing fairly well. She hired a jazz band (only Mummy could find a jazz band in the middle of Ethiopia). But why stop at one? She set up an orchestra in the house and a jazz band in the tent.

I was disappointed that this was mostly meant to be a grownup party, but Nursie took us out onto the grounds and let us peek in. The highlight came when Mummy got up on stage and started riffing with the band. She sang two songs, and the crowd reacted with applause and a lot of surprised and admiring laughter.

This was something new—Pat Korry, the new ambassador's wife, wasn't just a fine hostess, she was quite the entertainer! (In that era, ambassadors' wives were generally expected to behave like preacher's wives—quiet and dutiful.) My father loved that my mother wasn't dull and predictable like that, and I'm sure that night he was happy when people kept coming up to him and complimenting him on his glamorous and confident wife and telling him what a wonderful singer she was.

Still, there were repercussions. As much as Papa was proud of Mummy's creativity and talents, it turned out he was embarrassed by her performance. He didn't think it was seemly for an ambassador's wife to sing in front of her guests. In her previous life, she had danced the nights away (and probably sang up a storm) in the jazz clubs of Paris, but in Ethiopia, her career as a jazz artist was cut very short.

As for me, when I peeked into the tent I thought, "She looks so beautiful and elegant, just like Cinderella." She was a storybook figure to me, and just like a storybook figure, she was remote, perfect—and completely inaccessible.

I was much closer to another American woman who treated me with the attention and kindness I had hoped to find with my mother. This woman also happened to be one of the most unusual people I have ever met.

Jane Campbell was one of the first women hired to help manage the new Peace Corps. Jane, still in her twenties, worked in the Division of Volunteer Support, and became something of a legend in the Peace Corps in Ethiopia. We met because of her Peace Corps duties. As the ambassador's daughter, I was meeting "important people" all the time. Many of them were tiresome, and I could see right through their false friendliness as they strained to be nice to me just because I was the ambassador's daughter. Jane Campbell was one of the few people who was truly genuine.

Jane was legendary, because she possessed an eerie gift. Wherever she went, animals just came up to her. I don't mean just friendly little pet dogs either; birds of all sizes and shapes would flutter around her and land on her hand or shoulder; wild foxes would come up and trot beside her, and butterflies danced around her head ... it was a true gift. Animals were drawn to her home, and it became a compound for animals who came, like drawn to a magnet, to live with her. It became the grounds for more than a hundred wild animals, including elephants and lions.

Anyway, Jane found out that the ambassador's daughter loved animals as much as she did, and so she invited me to her living quarters and let me feed the lion cubs their milk from baby bottles. For a young girl like me, who was alienated in so many ways from the affection of my own family, the trust and acceptance from Jane Campbell, a vibrant young woman in her twenties, was unforgettable and deeply comforting.

Here is another gift from Ethiopia: A dozen years later, when I was in my mid-twenties, I was working in New York for UNICEF, which had just hired a new human resources head. We were encouraged to go to her office and introduce ourselves. Her name, Jane Beavan, didn't ring a bell, but something told me I knew her. All I knew was she lived in Connecticut, had quite a collection of animals, and had once lived in Africa.

When I got to her office door it was open, but she had somebody with her, and I was about to duck away again. But in that brief moment she glanced up, saw me at the door and instantly said, "Oh my God, it's Pat Korry's daughter Deborah!"

We had a beautiful reunion, right there on the spot, and exchanged a flood of memories.

Meeting Jane Campbell Beaven again was another gift Ethiopia gave me.

****

Today, Ethiopia is largely forgotten as a strategic power, but in the mid-twentieth century, under the rule of Emperor Haile Selassie, the country was a major player on the world stage and played a significant role in America's public policy. Naturally, that made it a go-to destination for American politicians.

In 1966, former Vice President Richard Nixon was gearing up for the 1968 presidential race, which meant making a fact-finding tour to Ethiopia, America's great strategic partner in Africa. One of the first things he did was ask to visit the largest outdoor bazaar in Addis. That impressed me because, as an eleven-year-old, that was what I would do if I came to visit Ethiopia! In other words, something fun and spontaneous and connected to the people. Nixon seemed genuinely interested in mingling with real Ethiopian culture.

My father arranged a tour of Addis for the former vice president, and as they were all getting ready to leave the embassy, I remember hanging around the periphery of the room as children do when something interesting is going on.

Suddenly, Nixon caught sight of me. He said, "Aren't your kids coming with us?"

My parents brushed it off, saying, "Oh, no, they will stay at home."

I never forgot Nixon's graciously impulsive gesture, and ever afterwards, despite all the political hatred he attracted in the Watergate years, I could never think of him without thinking of how genuinely he seemed interested in the Ethiopian people—and how kind he was for noticing a kid in the corner of the room.

Bobby Kennedy came to visit too, though not to visit any pungent outdoor bazaars or to meet the hoi polloi. It was also in 1966, a popular launch year for presidential contenders, and Kennedy came on a fact-finding tour of Africa as well. Ethiopia was his last stop. Bobby had already taken up his brother's torch, and he wanted to highlight his slain brother's founding of the Peace Corps, which was a major project in Ethiopia. The speech Bobby gave that day, all six pages of single-spaced, old-fashioned type, is now online.

In the speech, Kennedy praised Addis Ababa as "a vibrant center of African independence" and modernization, and he challenged the continent of Africa to take its part in preventing a nuclear holocaust, which was a familiar phrase back then. I was eleven and truthfully can't remember if I was there for the speech. What I do remember was Bobby Kennedy's visit also marked the launch of television in Ethiopia, and during his visit we plugged in our first TV set. If I remember correctly, it was hardly the launch of broadcast television. I think we had TV service only for one day.

Away from the podium and back at our residence, things loosened up. Bobby's wife, Ethel, was there, and she was very nice. What I remember most about her was that she was six months pregnant at the time, and probably because of that she couldn't decide what to drink. Despite the fact I was just a kid, I took it upon myself to ask Mrs. Kennedy for her drink preferences. Then I had to relay the drink request to one of the Ethiopian servants who brought her the drink, because I wasn't allowed to go to the kitchen to get it for her myself.

This convoluted ritual was made all the more complicated because Mrs. Kennedy was being so indecisive, and I kept sending the frazzled servant hiking back and forth from living room to kitchen, which was on the other side of our sprawling home.

"I'll have lemonade," Ethel said, and as soon as her lemonade arrived, "No, I think an iced tea would be better ..." and after a tall iced glass of tea was placed before her, "I think I would actually prefer a club soda!"

An old friend of Papa's, Sander Vanocur, was there too, because he was covering Bobby Kennedy on the campaign trail that year. "Sandy" Vanocur was like family—warm, friendly, and fun. He was the NBC White House correspondent when Jack Kennedy was president, and he and Papa were already good friends. They worked together in London and shared the experience of being American-born journalists (Sandy was born in Ohio), who had gone on to tackle adventurous careers overseas. When Papa first went to Washington to work for the Kennedy administration, Sandy Vanocur was one of the people who urged JFK to consider my father for the ambassadorship to Ethiopia.

I loved sitting in the corner of the room, listening to "Uncle Sandy" and Papa trade "war stories" about their days as journalists in London—Sandy at the Manchester Guardian, and Papa at UP and Look. Sandy Vanocur had a deep rich broadcaster's voice that bloomed and expanded into every corner of whatever room he was in, and it felt like home to have him there.

I will always consider Sander Vanocur part of our family, and in fact, he is. He is my sister Alexandra's godfather. I also remember that he dated the actress Shirley McLaine for a while, and on a visit to New York we stayed in her apartment for some reason. Frankly, I found it strange that Uncle Sandy would be dating her, because he didn't seem like someone who would be interested in Hollywood glamor types. As for me, I was never impressed by actresses or Hollywood. Even as a teenager, the glamor of it all was lost on me.

I soon forgot to worry about ever leaving Ethiopia. Of course, that was when everything was set in motion to change again. Back in Washington, President Johnson was implementing the "Korry

Report", my father's analysis of future American policy in Africa, and he was apparently impressed enough to want to offer my father advanced positions in his administration. He gave Papa three choices: The first was as director of the US Office of Fair Employment Practices; the second was to succeed Bill Moyers as Johnson's press secretary, and the third was the appointment as US Ambassador to Venezuela.

My father turned down all three.

Johnson was furious. According to a report attributed to Bill Moyers, the president had a fourth career choice for my father, which he delivered in an eighty-decibel voice:

"Then he can rot in hell in Ethiopia!"

My father's individualism and independence had run right up against Lyndon Johnson's legendary need for control. Well, my father also was very fond of his career in service to America and to an administration, and it didn't take long to realize he had made a misstep with a volatile and very proud president.

Months later, he saw his chance to redeem himself. He was in Washington with Emperor Selassie for another state visit, and at the end of a lavish White House dinner, my father pursued President Johnson up the grand staircase of the White House to make his pitch—and to make amends.

"Mr. President," he said, "I want you to know that I turned down your job offers because the best way I can serve you and my country is by being overseas, not in Washington."

Soon after Johnson promoted my father to Ambassador to Chile, which was considered a key Latin American post.

And so, Ethiopia ended for me after all. The country that began with "E" ended by being the country that formed me into the person I am.

To this day, moments and memories overtake me suddenly and make me realize that Ethiopia will always be with me. It may be a quick smile to an Ethiopian stranger in a New Jersey store, or sudden jolts of memory, like riding Whiskey into the hills of Addis, playing soccer on the embassy grounds, nudging baby bottles into the mouths of lion cubs, or the kindness of a powerful emperor with a fragile body and sad eyes.

But what mostly stays with me from Ethiopia is a deep perspective about life itself. After living closely with people who have so little, and who are immersed in true poverty, I have come to realize in a very profound way that I never, ever have a reason to complain about anything in life. I learned how the poorest, most abject human beings, who have so little in the way of material goods—not to mention food and water and basic health itself—still are able to express the greatest kindness and gentleness toward others.

Ethiopia also gave me a love for exploring the unknown, whether it be a foreign landscape or the human spirit of a stranger. And at no time was a person's color a consideration. This, too, was a gift from Ethiopia. I grew up truly color blind, in a way that is not possible in America. I never saw Ethiopians as being different than me because of their color. The same holds true for African Americans I meet, although here again, I see a disconnect in America that was not present in Ethiopia: black Americans are customarily called African Americans, even though their heritage may come from regions other than the continent of Africa.

Sometimes I sing under my breath a favorite song in Amharic, which was popular tune when we lived there. It speaks about the sorrow of saying goodbye to the people one loves, because it is time to go off to serve one's country. The words of the song, in Amharic or in English, might be about soldiers going off to war, but they also make me think of the sadness of being a young woman of twelve—already old beyond my years—and forced to leave a country I will never forget and will always love.

To this day the words, in Amharic, touch my soul: "Teregna negn ena, endatisheberi, Sileyish azanalehu, Almaz dehna ederi ..."

Translated, they are equally bittersweet:

"It is now my turn to give service, please don't be upset, I feel so sad to leave you ... good night!"

CHAPTER SIX

FROM BEAUTIFUL CHILE TO THE DEPTHS OF DESPAIR

Life is a series of adjustments. As an ambassador's daughter, I learned that lesson over and over again. Notably, when Ajax didn't turn up.

At first, I had other things to think about. I was packing boxes and deciding what to leave behind, because that was the life of an ambassador's daughter in October 1967. We were leaving Ethiopia. Papa got his marching orders from President Johnson to become the new ambassador to Chile.

I shook off my grief at losing Ethiopia by telling myself I was taking with me many of the things I loved best, including my German Shepherd dog, Ajax. I had no reason not to expect that Ajax would be one of the wonderful gifts from Ethiopia that I would be taking with me.

"Ajax will follow," Nursie promised me. Meanwhile, the journey to Chile itself crowded out all other thoughts—we took a boat from Miami, through the Panama Canal, and then on to Chile, a trip that transplanted me from the sub-Sahara to a new hemisphere and a new continent.

Santiago, Chile is encircled by the snow-capped Andes mountains and easy to love at first sight. I had never seen anything like it. We arrived in October, which meant summer was coming, because

Chile is in the southern hemisphere. Even in summer, the mountains stayed frosted with snow. For me, these new sights meant magical new adventures were ahead. There was no obvious poverty in Santiago, as there was in Addis Ababa. Santiago was modern, with beautiful shops, wide boulevards, sleek cars—and especially—happy-looking people, who were unburdened by poverty or mutilated limbs.

For Papa too, this was a new kind of professional adventure. Chile was an example of what the United States foreign policy hoped to encourage throughout South America. But the political climate was becoming more and more tense, which I'm sure also appealed to my father's sense of challenge (his cool nerves had landed him a job in post-war Yugoslavia, after all). Now, Marxist forces were making inroads in the Chilean government, and there were already rumblings that the country was on the verge of nationalizing the copper mines. The Johnson administration wanted a tough guy there to help negotiate and shepherd these inevitable changes through. My father had been successful in managing the delicate political balancing act in Ethiopia, and LBJ expected him to do the same in Chile.

Little did Papa know that other minefields were ahead for him—that had nothing to do with copper.

****

As for me, this was my fourth country. Two of them I loved in a special way—and for a lifetime. Ethiopia, with its surface poverty and harsh beauty, forced me to reach out with open arms and learn to love her, and when I did, I loved Ethiopia completely and could never, ever take it back. Chile was different—Chile offered its love quickly and recklessly like a handsome lover does, and it was impossible not to respond right away, like a grand and crazy love at first sight.

In the late 1960s, Chile already had a reputation: it was known for its three w's: wine, women, and weather. As a twelve-year-old, that translated into an energy and excitement that was rushing through Santiago in the late 1960s, like it was everywhere else in the modern world. Places like Haight Ashbury and Woodstock in the US, and Carnaby Street in London, were setting the pace for the whole era, and young people were leading the revolution. In Chile, there was the added buzz of cultures that made it a global crossroads: British, Lebanese, Syrians, and Germans were just some of the nationalities that were attracted to Chile for its powerful role in manufacturing, mining, and the textile industry.

In Ethiopia, my best friends were Ethiopians; in Chile, my world expanded into friendships with Chileans of many ethnic backgrounds. My best friend, Joyce Guler, was a Chilean of German descent. My first kiss, from my first boyfriend (in the days when boyfriend meant something more innocent than it does today), was from a Chilean with an English background. His name was Benjamin Cartwright. Ben was a wonderful first pololo (boyfriend). His family adored me as much as my family adored Ben, and for a long time we were inseparable. Ben was the only blond-blue-eyed man I've ever dated, and when he spoke English (rather than Spanish), it was with a wonderful British accent. Our innocent romance was interrupted by an American girl, who was eager to supply Ben's "needs" much faster than I was willing. But I didn't let it crush me; by then I was already learning to be self-reliant. My family had taught me, by default, to fend for myself.

Besides, Chile was too interesting to stay heartbroken (even in a minor key) for long. I soon realized I could love Chile without betraying my beloved Ethiopia, because they were so unlike each other. In Santiago, I remember riding a horse on the wet sands, with the blue Pacific roaring inches beside me and the hot sun beating down, and the waves and the spray slapping at my face. The cold shock of it was like life itself shouting at me, "Wake up, Deborah! Your time is coming!" I loved the icy water and the hot sun and the warmth of the people. I made friends right away, and I liked the fact that even the young people, like myself, were aware and knowledgeable about the world. I could talk to them about Ethiopia, because they were intelligent, knew about the country, and wanted to know more.

So, I fell in love with Chile, with the physical beauty of the country, the people, and the lifestyle. To this day, a part of my soul is totally Chilean. The friendships I made were the first true female friendships I ever had. Effortlessly, I embraced the Chilean-Latin American spirit, the language, and the music. It's become natural to me to express myself using my hands, and I think in an instinctive, intuitive way—all of which is thoroughly Latin. To this day, I am most at home in the Latin culture.

In Santiago, we had a private home on a hill with a winding drive and an ornate iron gate at the bottom of the street. The house was sleek and modern with lots of glass, curved corners and—as a grand flourish—big copper doors (a fitting touch, given that Chile is virtually built on copper). At the front of the house was a pool, and inside was a showcase of expressionist and abstract art. The Museum of Modern Art lent us 100 pieces. Everywhere you looked, you saw works by Rothko, Pollock, de Kooning, and Robert Morris. When you walked in the foyer, one of the first things you saw hanging from the ceiling was a slender original mobile by the American sculptor Alexander Calder, the artist who invented mobile art.

My mother was a painter too, and she was brave enough to hang her own work alongside these artist-greats. Santiago attracted many cultural and entertainment events, and the ambassador's residence became a favorite stop for many international artists who performed in the city. Duke Ellington, the great jazz pianist, came to Santiago for a concert series and ended up in our grand entrance hall, where he played jazz piano and Mummy sang. She floated around the house for days afterwards. Maybe having the chance to sing with Duke Ellington made up for her jazz career in Ethiopia being cut short.

It boggles my mind how easily I shrugged off all that privilege. When you're twelve and thirteen, you think every experience is equally interesting—and equally deserved. Besides, moving around so much, I had skipped grades easily, and by the time I got to Chile I was twelve going on twenty. But instead of making me inaccessible and arrogant, living with people of many cultures had done a good job of anchoring me in reality. I was unfazed about my father's job and way too down-to-earth to be snobbish about privilege or care what people thought. I didn't like to tell people where I lived, and I never gave people anything more than my first name (and certainly never offered my full name, Deborah Franklin Korry). I resisted adding Korry unless I absolutely had to, because by then the name of the US ambassador was well known throughout Chile.

By keeping my full name private, it was like having a delicious little secret: Only the people most in the know would make the connection, that my name linked two ambassadors born 200 years apart: Benjamin Franklin and Edward Korry.

****

"When is Ajax coming?" We had been in Chile for about six

months; I was too absorbed to be overly concerned, but really, it felt like it was time to ask about my dog! Of course, live animals had to be documented for travel, and there was all sorts of red tape to work out to bring Ajax to Chile. I understood that. But this seemed unusual. Was Ajax sick? Lost? Where was he?

Most of the questions fell on Nursie, and one day, so did the answer. She sat me down and said, in her brisk English way, "Ajax is not coming, and you will just have to get used to it."

Like many children who grow up as transplants, without settled roots, this was another example of learning to let things go; I had to adjust to new things quickly, and I could not to hold on to anything in life too tightly—and that included a family dog. Besides, I was used to my parents making decisions without concern for my feelings, but actually—by that time—I was way ahead of them about Ajax. What once was important, didn't seem to be anymore.

I started attending Santiago College, which was a private girls' school where we wore uniforms, as was the custom in all Chilean schools. Most of the students spoke English, but it was a Spanish school. In six weeks, I was speaking Spanish easily. I learned the language in rather a funny way—by watching three popular American television shows of the '60s which were translated into Spanish: Bonanza, Mission Impossible, and The Virginians.

To everyone but a trusted few, I never alluded to my family, and I hoped nobody would make the connection—"Oh, the ambassador's daughter!" If they did, I would never know if they wanted to be friends for me or my background.

On the surface things seemed calm, though far away from my troubles (as I learned later), the political situation was heating up, making it a constant diplomatic worry for the United States. Meanwhile, I went to school, did my homework, and interacted only occasionally with my parents, who were wrapped up in their own commitments. My older siblings had long since flown the coop, but it was easy to stay out of Alexandra and Nursie's way, because they had each other.

****

That very first year in Chile, all of a sudden Papa announced he had a conference in Aspen, Colorado, and I was to go with him— all by myself. (Well, not quite all by myself; my older sister, Kelly, was home from boarding school, and she was coming too. But no Mummy, no Nursie, no one else. Just Papa, Kelly, and me.

Papa had taken my brother Ted on a lot of trips (to France, Egypt, and Israel), and I think Mummy probably thought it would be good for him to spend more time with his daughters. I also think she had no idea how to keep us occupied in the summer. Frankly, I didn't care about the "why" of the trip. Even though I was trying to keep an air of cold detachment about everything having to do with my parents, secretly—in spite of myself—I was thrilled.

Papa's conference coincided with Aspen's famous annual classical music festival. The whole town (despite its trendiness, Aspen has always kept a cozy, small town feel) was lively and cheerful, with bright orange tents dotting the landscape. We spent a day listening to symphony orchestras perform in the open air, and then Papa surprised us with an orchestration of his own: a van was waiting for us, and we were headed for a huskie dog camp a few hours away.

When we arrived, an outdoors barbecue had been set up for visitors, but the main event was a concert composed of 150 singing huskie dogs. I could hardly fathom what that meant, but I was thrilled—overjoyed—to think something so magical was about to happen. Today, you can go on YouTube and hear huskies sing, but in the late '60s it was something pretty rare. The first chorus, of about seventy dogs, started to howl (in tune) to a piece that was instantly recognizable as the John Denver classic, "Rocky Mountain High". Swinging his baton, the owner asked Yogurt, one of his soloists, to start. The effect, with the chorus of other huskies backing Yogurt up, was magical and a little unearthly. The way these dogs were able to use their vocal chords was not at all like the weird wails of the hyenas in Ethiopia, because the hyenas' cries were anti-social and dangerous, while the huskies were singing melodiously, leaving me forever awestruck.

The huskies' trainer had given names to each dog. Banana, Cream, and Yogurt were the three soloists I remember. He called the troupe his boys and girls and divided them into sopranos and altos … and my twelve-year-old heart was completely captured. When I got back to Chile, I told myself, this is what I would do for the rest of my life. I was going to teach dogs to sing, and I was going to have my own chorus. I was going to travel the world and make people as happy as I was that day.

I was lost in this lovely idea when Papa announced it was time to leave Aspen.

"No, no—leave me! Please leave me here!" I'm afraid I made a little scene, but I couldn't help it. The singing huskies had filled up some aching and empty part of my heart. Maybe part of the lasting memory was because my father had made this magical event happen.

I never forgot that gorgeous afternoon in the Colorado mountains with the singing huskies. For years afterwards, I tried to find the troupe—I even ordered free-trial subscriptions of Colorado newspapers, hoping to find a mention of the man with the 150 singing huskies. But I never did.

When we got back to Chile, my parents decided to buy us a dog—but not just any dog, the best dog. I couldn't wait. For me, there was no lingering remorse over losing Ajax. When it came to dogs, I was a fickle lover. They found a breeder who specialized in offering the first purebred labrador retrievers to come to Chile; they were a championship breed from England. And so, we were joined by a heart-melting six-week-old puppy whom we named Principe Dorado de los Andes (Golden Prince of the Andes Mountains). We called him Prince.

I wasn't afraid at all to get close to Prince. Any previous attachments rolled off me easily. In other words, I was over Ajax.

****

Sometimes I wonder: When I begged to stay in Aspen with the singing huskies and made a little scene about it, was that was my eerie, extra-sensory intuition kicking in again? Because when we got back to Chile, although life went on, underneath the apparent normalcy, dangerous events were brewing that were going to change everything.

Political activist Salvador Allende had been running for president of Chile for thirty years and always lost. But Allende, a physician by training, never quit. By the late '60s, he had grown enough in power that he was considered a serious contender. He was a founder of a socialist faction in the country and had strong international Marxist ties, including with the Soviet Union. Naturally, that alarmed the United States.

In 1968, the Allende problem had been inherited by the new president, Richard Nixon. Of course, every ambassador serves the pleasure of the president, so Papa didn't know if he had a job much longer. In fact, Nixon liked my father (they got to know each other when Nixon, then a political outcast, had visited our embassy in Ethiopia). Besides everything else, Nixon knew my father was good at his job—and he had guts. Those were especially good qualities at the time, because it was taking more and more courage to be a diplomat in Chile.

One day, a car careened up to our street-level gate house and opened fire on our guards. There was a hail of bullets and the rat-a-tat of gunfire. In the house, we all froze. The winding drive from the gate house leading up to our home suddenly seemed very, very short.

Then the thugs sped away, and the guards, who weren't hurt, called the house and reported to my father, "Those guys were out to kill you and your whole family."

The governments of Chile and the US wanted to increase security around our home, but that would have essentially turned our property into a military outpost.

"Absolutely not!" my father said. "If they're gonna get us, they'll get us. But you're not making us live that way." Still, ominous changes had to be made. Papa went to work every day in his chauffeur-driven car. But then, his route and his departure schedule were changed-up regularly, and he even altered the places where he sat in the car.

As for me, I never worried; I simply didn't give a damn.

However, my youthful courage (if that's what it was) didn't save me from events. One night in September 1969, after my father got home from work, he and my mother sat me down and delivered an announcement: I was to leave Chile the very next morning to continue school in upstate New York.

That fast.

They always insisted the reason had nothing to do with the

growing political violence. No, they said, the reason was that Nursie was complaining that I was a bad influence on Alexandra! Nursie was having a hard time controlling me. (Leave it to my family to feel more threatened by family dissension than by the prospect of a violent government overthrow). I was horrified, and utterly unprepared for this devastating news.

My parents put it this way: "Well, Nursie feels you have become too difficult and combative, and we can't have this situation continue. So, either Nursie goes or you have to go, and we've decided it's best that you go."

"But I don't want to leave!"

"The decision is made," they said. "You're on a plane tomorrow; you'll be going to New York. Grandpa will pick you up and make arrangements to get you to school in upstate New York."

"But I want to say goodbye to my friends!"

"We're sorry, Deborah, but that cannot happen."

Years later, when I was in my mid-forties, I was visiting my parents and decided to ask the question that I had never asked before. I hadn't been brooding over it; I was simply curious. Mummy was at the sink, and Papa was sitting at the table with me when I asked, "Why?"

"Why did you decide that it was best for me to leave, instead of Nursie?" (Maybe my memory had been wrong; maybe they hadn't meant to hurt me like that ...)

Papa replied to my question right away. "Actually, it was your mother's idea," he said. "I told her after we left New York that we didn't need Nursie anymore, we should just hire local people when we went to different places. But she wanted the continuity of the same person; she thought it would be important, especially for Alexandra."

At that, Mummy turned from the sink impatiently, as if to say this was an old argument she thought had been settled long ago. "That's not true, Ed!" she said. "We made the decision together!"

And that's how the matter was left—I was in exactly the same place I was in at age twelve. It was hardly a shock that my parents weren't willing to be honest and straightforward with me. And besides, for years I had known the real reason for sending me away—Nursie was more important to keep than I was. Even after all those years, I was just curious to know whether either parent would admit the truth. In a way, my father did. My mother still couldn't. Anyway, the past is the past.

But that's how I ended up at the Emma Willard School in Troy, New York.

****

I arrived at Emma Willard just two months shy of my fourteenth birthday. My arrival began what I would remember as the worst experience of my young life.

Emma Willard School was—and still is—a legendary boarding school and preparatory academy for girls that dates back to 1821. The main buildings are as grand as those at any university, done in stately Gothic style, and the campus itself sits on a high point called Mount Ida, which overlooks Troy, NY.

The setting was gorgeous: the memories, pure misery. I can sum up the whole drab, dispiriting beginning of it all with this one depressing image: Grandpa Korry dropping me off at the Greyhound bus terminal at the Port Authority of New York, on 42nd Street and 8th Avenue. Soon I was on a bus, all alone, heading for Emma Willard.

Years later, I came across letters my mother wrote to my grandmother about sending me there: "A somewhat traumatic decision all the way around," my mother wrote. "For me, it's a great load off my mind, especially at this particular time, because we are going through a very trying period and will continue to do so for quite a while."

In another letter she wrote: "Deborah writes frequently from the depths of despair."

Yes, I was in the depths of despair—and for good reason.

It wasn't just that I disliked upstate New York, or that I missed Chile. No, it was a lot of things, including the fact that the hangings started again.

****

I didn't like my roommate, Sarah, at all. She was unfriendly and appeared—in my perception—to be on drugs. She was of average height, with a sandy brown pixie haircut, and the only immediately memorable thing about her was that she arrived at Emma Willard by helicopter. Sarah's family had made its fortune in the ski industry, but there was nothing about this sullen and silent person that suggested anything as healthy and invigorating as outdoor sports.

I quickly summed up the possibilities of friendship as pretty hopeless.

Anyway, school was supposed to start Monday, and I decided to concentrate on that.

I went to sleep, and when I woke up, I had that groggy sensation of being in a strange place: that common waking-up moment when you're not quite sure where you are—or what's real.

But this time, there was something else.

I tried hard to focus, because at first I could not believe what I was seeing: Sarah's body was hanging over me. She had tied herself to the exposed pipes in the high ceiling of our room and killed herself.

Whatever people expect someone in my position to do, I didn't do it. I didn't scream or faint; I simply went out in the hallway to get someone on staff to take her body down. People weren't worried about how I was; this was long before the era of PTSD diagnoses and grief counseling. Everyone simply noted how calm I was, and therefore, they thought I was just fine. My life was expected to go on, and I was not reassigned to another room. Later, they moved in a girl who cried all the time.

In the dark, as I tried to go to sleep, I tried not to think about what had happened there and to wonder why I had been sent to this awful school.

Then, a few weeks later, blood started to appear in random beds, and in the bathrooms. The word "pig" was written in blue across the tile walls of the bathroom and across the mirrors. This was soon after the Sharon Tate murders that had shocked the whole country in the summer of '69, so everyone thought Charles Manson's influence had now spread to our prestigious girls' school. The dean of students, a woman by the name of Ms. Spears, decided to round up the girls she thought might be responsible for these atrocities. I was one of them.

I had attracted suspicion, apparently, because I behaved too calmly after awaking to find my roommate hanging from the ceiling of our room. (What is the proper way to react to such an event?) We four suspects were moved to the infirmary, supposedly to keep a better eye on us. Occasionally, we were allowed back to our rooms to pick up clothes and other personal materials and—of course— every time we were allowed to do so, more blood was found in more beds and in the bathrooms.

As I recall, eventually the FBI was called in and the culprits were found: they were two day students who had access to animal blood in one of their father's science labs.

But the damage was done.

I was told I had grounds to bring a lawsuit against Emma Willard, but as a fourteen-year-old, what did I know about lawsuits? My parents weren't much help either; I learned that when Papa and Mummy were told I was under suspicion, their reply was, "We support whatever the school thinks appropriate." They explained to the school officials that I had been a difficult, combative child at home; perhaps I had other issues they were not aware of?

I was too disassociated from my parents to lament such apparent disloyalty; for me, their cool detachment was exactly the climate I grew up in. What kept me from losing my grip at Emma Willard was, literally, keeping a tight grip on my guitar. It was a handsome, handmade guitar, inlaid with fine wood. I had been given the guitar in Chile, where I took lessons from a wonderful old blind man who was gentle and kind. Those were the memories I focused on.

At every chance, I would go off by myself, and play all the music of my era—some Dylan, a lot of Joan Baez tunes, and definitely everything by Carole King, which I loved the best. Years later, in my 50s, when I connected on Facebook briefly with two old colleagues from my Emma Willard days, they told me that what they remember most about me was seeing me off by myself, playing my guitar, and they'd wonder what I was thinking so intensely about. They didn't know it, but what I was doing was … keeping a grip on things.

Relief came when I went back to Chile for the summer.

That summer, something happened in Chile that seemed to prove I was being followed by malignant spirits: my mother discovered our maid, Elena, hanging dead in a closet of our home. I heard Mummy screaming, and I ran toward the noise and saw Elena hanging there, blackened and sickening.

Elena was a very gentle person, unmarried, with a six-year-old daughter who adored her. She was a person of darker color, which in Chile made her an object of prejudice, so it was unlikely she would ever get ahead in life. Because she was dark-skinned and had a child out of wedlock, even the staff shunned her. Elena was a good person, and so shy and quiet, it was hard to fathom that she could commit such a violent act—to hang herself.

My mother liked Elena and was trying to get her papers to come to America where she could keep working for the Korry family. But instead of helping her get to America, it was Mummy's sad fate to find Elena when she went to the closet to rummage for her golf clothes.

****

Are hangings going to follow me for the rest of my life?

Of course, there was no answer to that question—not then, anyway—and life kept pushing ahead. Unknown to me, I was being propelled by undercurrents I couldn't see at the time. In my case, after my summer in Chile, I was being sent back to Emma Willard for further punishment. My heart was dead inside, too numb to do anything but drift with the tide, and somehow wait for a way to get back to Chile, my friends, and a country I loved.

There's a postscript to this story, which I think shows how many secrets, and how much suffering, lives inside of each one of us— without anyone else having a clue. Just a few years ago, a student from Emma Willard's found me on Facebook.

"Oh, Deborah, do you remember me from Emma Willard: the

best school in the whole wide world!" she wrote. "I want to send you a package of pictures of you playing your guitar."

All I could think was, "Oh god ... I don't want to see any pictures or remember anything from that time."

CHAPTER SEVEN

A GIRL WHO GREW UP ALL OVER THE WORLD

The pain of Emma Willard lasted for sixteen months. As soon as possible I moved on to Chevy Chase School in Bethesda, Maryland—and from there to George Washington University.

Given my life experiences, I figured a degree in international relations would be the challenge I needed—just the opposite was true. I listened to lectures on Africa and didn't recognize the continent. The professors could have been describing the state of Ohio. The basic information was accurate, but I had already studied it by the ninth grade. The part where I had actually lived? It bore little resemblance to what the professors opined. What a waste, I said to myself. I knew they couldn't teach me anything new, and even worse, I knew that I knew more than they did.

That's when I realized I held the key to my future in my own hands, and that was financial independence, not the fiction I was being taught at George Washington University. I found a nice apartment near the Watergate Hotel, and pretty soon I was working as a hostess at the Key Bridge Marriott in Virginia and making $1,000 a week in cash, which was huge money at the time. I was cocky enough to be glad I was making more than my professors.

For the first time, life was coming easy to me. Only years later did I re-evaluate my arrogance and realize I had probably cheated myself by not staying at George Washington, which has a highly-regarded international relations school. But at the time, I was making a lot of money; the goal of earning a law degree, or pursuing a future in politics, wasn't a priority. Still, I have to ask myself—how different would things have been if I had gone to law school? And after that, who knows?

Through all that time, I stuck with my rule of never telling anyone I was an ambassador's daughter. My father was a journalist. That was my story. Funny, my mother was the dramatic opposite. At every turn, she managed to slip in the fact that, "My husband was the ambassador ..." She thrived on his titles and position.

As for me, I was very happy to work incognito as a hotel hostess. This was the 1970s, and my work clothes were red suede hot pants, a little white shirt with a snappy red suede vest, and white go-go boots. It was a silly outfit, but I was a good hostess—professional and focused. Bill Marriott, the scion of the family's hotel chain, was famous for his "management by walk-around" style, and when he came into the Key Bridge to nose around the premises, he would stay for a drink and often leave me $100 tips, so I knew I was a good employee.

I was pretty happy there, until one night a customer grabbed my shirt and ripped it open. I pulled away and slapped him—and was fired on the spot. The era of sexual harassment charges and lawsuits was still in the future. At this time, women weren't taken seriously, and support from the hotel staff was nonexistent.

So, I did what I suppose kids with nowhere to go have been doing from time immemorial—I moved in with my parents. By then they were living in Briarcliff Manor, a pretty village in Westchester County, about thirty miles outside New York City. How my parents ended up in a conventional setting after all their overseas adventures is a story in itself. Whatever injustice I faced at the hotel chain, or in being passed over for later jobs, was nothing compared to the injustice coming my father's way, as I will explain in due time.

****

As for me, I wanted to break away from the conventional path and forge my own way, very much like Papa had. In the meantime, I couldn't have been further from that goal. What could be more conventional than living with my parents and going to the famous Katharine Gibbs Secretarial School? For decades, the name Katharine Gibbs radiated discipline and propriety. Its curriculum was designed to attract college women and to prepare them for excellent support jobs in the business world.

Secretarial school was hardly my life's grand vision, but I was being lashed forward by a harsh warning from my father which I have never forgot: "Deborah, if you don't do something with your life, you're going to end up being an elevator boy—and they're not going to call you Deborah, they're going to call you Frankie. And you're going to be hoisting people up and down a building all day, and they won't say a word to you except 'Fifth floor, Frankie,' and 'Lobby, please, Frankie.' What kind of life is that?"

The sheer horror of being an androgynous elevator boy in white gloves, pulling levers and opening metal doors all day so other people could step out into their own exciting lives—well, that was enough to drive me forward.

For a while, my path was a daily slog, but I can't complain because it led me to the United Nations International Children's Emergency Fund (UNICEF), which became my haven. Ironically, UNICEF's mission—to rescue lost and suffering children—might have served a hidden purpose in rescuing me.

UNICEF was founded in 1946 to help suffering children in postwar countries. By 1953, UNICEF's mandate was extended to address the needs of all children in the developing world.

My job was as program assistant to the Middle East Division. Fuad, my boss, was an Iranian-born writer and intellectual who spoke five languages. Fuad was of Russian and Lebanese descent and truly a citizen of the world. He was director of Middle East programs, and together, Fuad and I started UNICEF News, a newsletter for employees around the world to share stories of their experiences and projects with the rest of the UNICEF family.

Fuad was my first mentor, and he turned UNICEF into my home. Finally, I was working with people who had been raised all over the world: who spoke multiple languages and had a similar interest in and understanding of the world. We all were there to use our experiences and talents to help others. For the first time in my life, I felt I totally belonged. Until then, I was a girl who grew up all over the world, and yet I belonged to no country, no person, and no family.

Was I American? No, I never felt so. I was Chilean, I was Ethiopian, and I was a citizen of the planet—just like Fuad! When I met young women my own age, but outside of our UNICEF world, I couldn't relate to their cultural customs, because it was like stepping into another foreign country. When they started talking about the latest "hot" place to meet after work, or where they got their nails done, I just looked at them with a blank stare.

Fuad gave me a home base and built my confidence. He was the first person in my life to recognize and appreciate my talents. He made me feel there wasn't anything I couldn't do—and he challenged me to do it. He liked my writing style and gave me many program reports to work on. He handed me projects above and beyond my experience—because he knew I could handle them. All of a sudden, I had this wonderful boss who had no children of his own, who was willing to take me on like his daughter. For me, he was in many ways that missing piece of my father that I had never managed to bring to life.

Of course, happiness is rarely permanent. The day came too soon when Fuad announced he was leaving, because he was going to head UNICEF's new office in post-war Vietnam. I didn't want to stay in my present job and work for anyone else but Fuad. So, I applied for a position in a continent that was already steeped in my bones: Africa.

To my shock, even though Fuad lobbied on my behalf, I was turned down. The response from UNICEF was that a young American woman like me couldn't be assigned to a field office in Africa. I was devastated. I had lived on three continents, spoke three languages, and had been in the thick of Ethiopia's culture and politics since I was a child—but I didn't qualify to go to Africa? UNICEF was filling positions in Africa with people from every country in Europe—who had never been outside their home countries!

As much as I loved UNICEF, with Fuad gone, it was as if the curtain had been pulled away from all the good works of the organization. I could see the bureaucratic machine grinding away behind the draperies. It represented a stiff, soulless bureaucratic world I didn't want to be a part of, and I resigned.

Why, why was I so stubborn? I had been offended by one setback, only because I didn't get the job in Africa! For some time afterwards, I mourned leaving such a great organization, where we were all truly helping people in a practical way. Every child, from every country, was worthy of UNICEF's attention. We weren't a money-handout organization either; we were built on the philosophy that people value something more when they have created it and built it themselves. After all, I was the one who had written the stories for UNICEF's newsletter about my colleagues' joy and satisfaction when they went into remote towns where there was no running water, and they trained local people to sink water wells and build homes. This was important work.

I kicked myself over and over again for deciding to leave, and then it hit me—except for the details, I was acting out—pretty much in the mirror image of my father: He had quit UP with only four months to go to get his pension. Why? Because "They want to change my story!" I had to face the fact that I had quit a job of my dreams for a similarly stubborn need to take a stand—at the expense of my own settled happiness.

But maybe that's the key: neither my father nor I ever could stand to settle for anything, even happiness.

I lost contact with Fuad for twenty years or so and then reconnected with him while working in New York in 2007. He was retired and living in Canada, but still involved with UNICEF, and he never lost that graciousness that made him one of the nicest human beings I've ever known.

In recent years, I received a beautiful letter from him that was both dignified and spirited, and explained, straight from his heart, that I meant a great deal to him. I read and re-read the letter and was struck by something I had never realized: All those years before, in his quiet and unobtrusive way, Fuad had been there for me, when I was a sister, a friend, and a daughter—with no family to love.

****

Like a lot of bright people who spend too much time in the service world, I was an easy mark for the demon that whispers in the ear, "C'mon, Deborah, you're smart and talented and you deserve a flashy career where you can make some real money." In other words, it was time to enter the private sector, and I did—not at a walk, but at a run.

I joined a small, old-money law firm as a legal assistant, where I learned the secrets of off-shore investments and saw firsthand the effects of that great '70s past-time—snorting cocaine. The firm was owned and run by two individuals. One was a fellow in his 30s, from a prestigious Virginia family of impeccable Anglo-Saxon pedigree; the other was a diminutive, deeply insecure man of Jewish ancestry in his early 50s.

The younger man, the Virginian, was also a raving lunatic who spent most of the work day standing at his desk snorting nose candy. But it wasn't just him; it turned out that the carpeted calm, the expensive artwork on the walls, and the hushed tones of the well-trained receptionists were just fronts that hid a pile of chaos. When I walked into a meeting room, there would often be lines of cocaine on the table and the raving Virginian would call out, as naturally as if offering me coffee, "Hey Deborah, come in and have some!"

I was young, but I was smart-young; I never wanted to get involved.

When it came to drugs and men, I think my aloofness and independence saved me from the worst of mistakes. But who could fully escape the 1970s? Either you fell into its traps, or you learned to inch your way around them.

No one can hold the world at bay for long. While at UNICEF I met Aleussia, a woman who worked as secretary to the head of UNICEF; she was looking for a roommate. Aleussia and I had a lot in common; she was a Venezuelan American who traveled all over the world on UNICEF business, so she spoke Spanish and English like I did. Our conversations were like a fast-moving verbal tennis matches, pinging back and forth in two languages.

One night, Costas, a close Greek friend of Aleussia's (who by then was my roommate), arranged for us to go and meet up with a number of his Greek sailor friends who were in New York for Fleet Week. (This event is a festive pause on the military calendar, in which ships that have recently returned from overseas dock in various cities. The sailors get a chance to visit the local sights, and the public is treated to ship tours and military displays.)

Anyway, the local sights arranged for our Greek visitors consisted of dinner at Estias, a famous Greek restaurant up on the Upper East Side. At some point, Aleussia and Costas excused themselves to use the restrooms. I was so naive, I thought they were really using the restrooms. It wasn't long before they were back, and I didn't think anything of it.

Later that night, when I went to the restroom, Costas was waiting for me in the corridor.

"Do you want to see something interesting in the meat freezer?" he said.

I had heard dumb lines from men before, but that was a first.

"Well … not really," I said. He pressed the issue, but he did it so good-naturedly; I admit I was amused and intrigued. So, I agreed to go with him to a huge walk-in freezer where huge slabs of lamb and who-knows-what-else meats were dangling from hooks. Costas rummaged around like he had been there before, and then pulled out a small plastic bag which contained a pinkish colored rock, which I quickly was informed was cocaine. The little I knew about cocaine was from the movies, and I had always thought it was white in color. Now I was getting an education, which included the fact that pure cocaine is the color pink.

Costas said, "Do you want to try some?"

"You're crazy—no way!"

"You lived in South America, and you never tried cocaine?"

I said, "No."

And he said, "Well, you know Aleussia did it with me."

Gee, I lived with Aleussia, and I had no idea she had tried cocaine! Besides, I had just seen Aleussia upstairs, and she looked perfectly fine. I thought about it a little and figured, *How terrible could it be?* If Aleussia did it, I could do it.

"Okay, I'll try it." He tapped out cocaine from the plastic bag onto a rolled piece of paper money (maybe a twenty-dollar bill) and said, "Now, stick it in your nostril and inhale."

On the first try, he didn't tell me to hold the other nostril, and it all flew away.

The second time, I did something wrong again.

"You are very expensive," he said.

The third time was better, and we went back upstairs. At first, I thought Aleussia looked very normal, as did Costas. Then things started to kick in. I noticed their teeth were chattering, and so were mine, and then I noticed Aleussia was much more talkative than usual. Then I started to feel odd. When we got back to the apartment, the cocaine continued to flow. By then, I was in full-fledged energy mode. It was 4:30 a.m., and though I was aching for sleep, I was flayed by a weird energy that I wanted to shake off but couldn't. As the effects slowly drained away—twenty-four to thirty-six hours later—I thought, *What a waste of time!* From then on, I looked at people who used cocaine—my roommate and my bosses—with complete puzzlement and even a little bit of awe. I didn't see how they could do it and stay functional.

Eventually, Aleussia passed from my life as a roommate, even though we stayed friends. I was less lucky with my next roommate.

Lee was a flight attendant with Pan Am. She seemed nice, and so we found a place. When you're young—at least in those days—you didn't ask a prospective roommate for a resume and five references. Lee was gone a lot, which was good; but she had highly creative ways of avoiding paying rent, which was bad. Her great service to me was to introduce me to Kari Anne, who was originally from Norway, and who has become one of my closest lifelong friends.

Honest, loyal, caring Kari Anne must have been the universe's benevolent payback for having to live with Lee.

Besides mooching on the rent, when Lee returned from her overseas trips, she was a carouser, always ginning up the next party. I would come home from work and slip in my bedroom to get away from the din and marijuana smoke, but you can't really get away from anything if you're living in an apartment in New York. The next day, I would wake up bleary-eyed from lack of sleep, but the place was always clean. Lee was gone, leaving behind little notes that said things like, "I'm flying to Paris, back in five days."

We had a glass bowl in the middle of the table in the living area, and one day I noticed in a vague sort of distracted way that it was filled with something. Almost on cue, cops were banging on the door.

"We have a warrant," they said, and asked for my roommate by name.

Suddenly—it was like a slap to the head—I put two and two together and then my self-preservation kicked in. Through a crack in the door I said my roommate was away, but I would be right there. I grabbed that big bowl, sitting so innocently on the table, and raced to the bathroom. It felt like a hundred years before I was able to flush that avalanche of white cocaine down the toilet.

The cops came in, and I don't know if they weren't trying too hard, or Lee's general tidiness around the apartment had thrown them off—or I maybe was just very good at flushing cocaine down the toilet. In any case, they asked me a few questions and left. No big deal.

But when Lee got back it turned into a very big deal. In between the tongue lashings, I learned I had flushed $10,000 worth of quality cocaine into the New York City sewer system. Her boyfriend had given it to her for safekeeping, and she let me know he was going to be seriously unhappy about this.

"And what are you going to do about it?" she yelled at me.

I had no money; my days were marked. Shortly afterwards, I came home from work and found my whole apartment cleaned out.

I looked at my apartment key, and then looked at the blank walls and completely empty spaces everywhere between them. I was confused. Had my key opened the door to the wrong apartment? Slowly I grasped the truth: Lee had taken her revenge. The doorman told me that all day long people had been coming in and out, hauling away furniture, lamps, hangers of clothes, and heavy bags. Lee sold everything. All she left for me was her phone bill for $2,700—and three months of unpaid rent.

****

Men were a simpler problem. With men, I knew I was an enigma, even intriguing. A lot of men were tired of the hot pants and go-go boots set, so I didn't even have to try to be different, it was enough to share some of my experiences, like riding my horse along the beaches of Chile or hearing hyenas call from outside my window in Addis Ababa. For a lot of men, hearing about those experiences was a lot sexier than thigh-high hemlines. Plus, I gathered that I was—as they say—"easy to look at", though I didn't feel that way about myself at all. Was I attractive? Unlike a lot of women, I was indifferent to the idea, but I was willing to assume that some men found me so. Yet I couldn't shake the happiness-scorching notion that if my father didn't love me and my mother didn't love me, what are the chances that this person will really and truly love me?

So, while I accepted the attention and the devotion, somewhere inside of myself I was saying in a subconscious way, "Yeah, right. I wonder how long this is going to last!" In effect, I spit out men; I broke a lot of hearts. And I didn't have to sleep with them either, to do it—they were simply, hopelessly enamored, because they built up in their minds this magical story of being with a girl who grew up all over the world.

Most of those men are long forgotten, but not all.

I hated blind dates, but Aleussa's friend, Ronald, set me up with a friend of his, Steve. I liked what I heard during our early phone conversations, so why not? For our first date, Steve was waiting for me in his car. Wanting to show my independence, I slipped into the passenger seat without waiting for him to help. Immediately I was struck by this handsome guy—a dream blind date! We arrived at an Italian restaurant, and he pulled the car right to the front door, as if it's his own parking space. "Why don't you get out," he said. "There's a lot of traffic."

At that point I wondered—why isn't he getting out of the car himself?

Then he turned around and began fussing with something mechanical and heavy in the back seat. It was a wheelchair.

Now, some girls might have panicked, but I had lived side by side with people with leprous, missing limbs; I grew up not expecting people to be conventionally perfect. "Can I help?" I asked, but Steve was cheerful and confident, brushed me off, and got himself in the chair. Inside the restaurant, he was greeted as an old friend, and we were both treated like royalty.

From that night on, Steve and I clicked. We saw each other for about two months, and shared simple, tender intimacies and long, lovely kisses. I admired him from the start, because there was something good and wholesome about him. Later, I learned that Steve's All-American looks weren't just for show—he had been a star athlete and just starting out on a football scholarship at a major university. The first day of football practice, he broke his neck. Though permanently paralyzed, he went on to complete his education, and he graduated with his class from his hospital bed. An awesome man.

Steve was never bitter; instead, he was always worried about me. "You deserve a vacation," he told me one night. I was exhausted by work, but I brushed him off. He persisted. It turned out he really meant it—he wanted to send me on a vacation. He couldn't go because of his work, he said. After some more protests I accepted his kind gift and went to the island of Eleuthera in the Bahamas for five days, all by myself.

In our few short weeks together, we shared—and maybe healed—two lifetimes' worth of memories, hurts, and disappointments. We discovered a mutual love of the poem: "If" by Rudyard Kipling. "If you can keep your head when all about you ..."

But I couldn't sustain the weight of our shared lives. I was in my twenties, still restless and wondering what was beyond the next hill. I couldn't see myself getting serious about anyone, and I knew I couldn't handle the commitments necessary to bring happiness to a man in a wheelchair.

Only one thing was left to do: I broke Steve's heart.

Steve answered my halting explanation with no bitterness, no anger, no "whys?" He accepted my announcement as if he was expecting it. After all, he had suffered far worse. A while later, after the shock had worn off, we got together for a gentler farewell, and he surprised me with a present.

"I know you don't want to go out anymore, but I want to give you this," he said. It was the poem "If", beautifully framed, the words written out in bold calligraphy.

Steve was the best of the best. I knew it would tear open a huge wound if we tried to stay in touch, yet he is a memorable person in my life. I just knew it wouldn't work. Our time together had been complete. There was no need to wonder what it would have been like … if?

****

I met my first husband because of Aleussia too. It was only a few months after Steve and I stopped dating. Aleussia and I were having a girls-only night out in a restaurant when our table was besieged by a darkly handsome fellow and his friends. Johnny (as I'll call him) was a character—I referred to him as Mr. Greek American Playboy. He was everything I couldn't stand—and I married him anyway.

Johnny was ten years older than I and ready (so he said) to get married. He also said he was the nephew of Aristotle Onassis, the shipping magnate. Johnny was enormously flirtatious, slightly dangerous, and wickedly challenging, and I fell for all of it. He became part of our little group and cultivated the reputation of being a real ladies man who had dated 300 women, but the only woman he wanted to marry was …. me! How lucky could I be?

Today I laugh, but that's only to keep from crying over how stupid I was. I knew he wasn't the right person to marry. But he was a salesman—and a good one—and he should have gotten a national award for the sales job he did on me. He convinced me we absolutely needed to buy a condo in New Jersey, we needed to buy boats and Jaguars so he could work on them, and we needed (eventually) to buy a house.

The catch was Uncle Aristotle had apparently not shared his wealth with Johnny, so all our "needs" had to be financed from my good credit—and out of my savings account. But I was happy and recklessly in love. Above all, Johnny loved life—he wasn't a drinker or a druggie or a gambler, he was simply high on himself, and that made it easy for me to get high on him. His good humor and sunny irresponsibility was literally intoxicating. Besides, he expressed his love openly and lavishly, which was so different from the bare-cup-board variety I had grown up with at home.

We married on September 11, 1982, on a yacht on the Hudson River. My parents came to the wedding but didn't stay long, and their analysis of Johnny was brutal.

"He's a bullshit artist," Papa said.

By October, friends were telling me they had seen Johnny in some of our favorite restaurants, fooling around with girls.

The future Ambassador Edward Korry, Papa, sitting on a New York beach with his parents, Samuel and Gertrude Korry, circa 1928

My maternal grandparents, New York Governor Nathan Miller and his wife, Elizabeth Davern, circa 1937 celebrating the christening of the "N.Miller" steamship, built by his friend Andrew Carnegie in his honor.

My parents' wedding day, July 7, 1950. The wedding was held in a Catholic church in Syracuse, N.Y. even though my father was agnostic.

8 Villa Spontini, Paris, France where I spent my first childhood years. My mother drew this sketch and highlighted our home, circa 1956. Papa was working for United Press International.

Papa and me on the beach in Costa Grava, Spain 1957. A rare
family vacation and display of Papa's affection towards me.

With my siblings in Ennismore Gardens, our London home, circa
1959. Kelly is on the left, Ted and I in the foreground, Alexandra on
Mummy's lap and Papa sitting on the arm chair. Papa was working for
Look Magazine.

With President Kennedy in the Oval Office 1963, following the swearing in of my father as ambassador to Ethiopia. Left to right, Mummy, Alexandra, me. Ted, Kelly and my maternal grandmother, Mildred McCarthy.

Historic moment: the new United States ambassador to Ethiopia and his wife (Mummy and Papa) stepping off the plane in Addis Ababa, 1963. Two of my siblings and I were right behind them.

Our home in Addis Ababa, The American Embassy residence. A very large yet warm and inviting home filled with furniture and artwork my parents collected from all over the world.

Papa in top hat and coattails on his way to present his diplomatic credentials to Emperor Haile Selassie, 1963. Ted, me, and Alexandra are in front of Mummy and Papa.

Meeting Emperor Haile Selassie at the Palace 1963. Mummy,
Alexandra, me, followed by Kelly.

The Lion of Judah with his beloved chihuahua, Lulu.

From left, Kelly, Ted, me, and Alexandra in front of our house in Ethiopia, circa 1966. A rare photo of all 4 siblings as Kelly and Ted were attending boarding schools in Europe.

On top of "Korry Mountain," the 9,000-foot peak outside of Addis Ababa where our family went on an occasional picnic, circa 1965. This is where I lost my eyesight in one eye for a period of time.

Bobby Kennedy, gearing up to run for President, came to Ethiopia with NBC Correspondent Sander Vanocur, 1966. From left, "Sandy" Vanocur, Sen. Bobby Kennedy, Alexandra sitting on Kennedy's lap, Mummy in back, and me on the right. "Uncle Sandy" played a lead role in my father being named an ambassador.

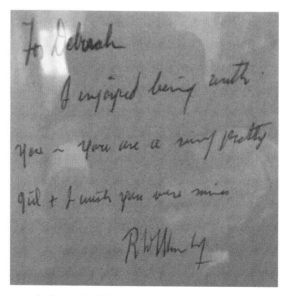

A personal autograph from Bobby Kennedy. "I enjoyed being with you. You are a very pretty girl and I wish you were mine". His words deeply moved me as he and his wife Ethel were expecting their 10th child.

Our handsome, loyal, horse groom Sa'id. He was my trusted companion on our gallops into the hills of Addis Ababa.

Our Ethiopian limousine driver, Fanta, with his children. My daily driver to school.

Our embassy staff and their children. These were my friends and playmates. Some lived, some were imprisoned and some executed during the Marxist coup that toppled the Selassie regime.

Mummy and Papa with Richard Nixon who was visiting Ethiopia before his presidential run, circa 1966.

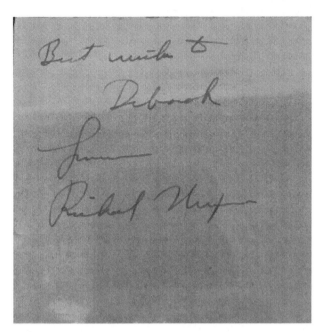

Nixon's personal autograph to me. I treasure this note as he was very kind
to me. Though my parents said no, he invited me to tag along with my
parents to see the Merkato, the largest open air market in Africa.

Haile Selassie and Papa with JFK, Washington, DC, October 1963.
Haile Selassie was the last major head of state to visit Washington
before President Kennedy was assassinated one month later.

Haile Selassie with Papa at the White House reception given by
President Lyndon Johnson and Lady Bird, circa 1966

Papa's swearing-in ceremony as Ambassador to Chile at the State Depart-
ment, 1967. Left to right: Radomiro Tomic (Chilean Ambassador to the
US), me, Secretary of State Dean Rusk, Sen. Bobby Kennedy, Alexandra,
Mummy, and my father.

The front of our house, the American Embassy residence, in Chile, 1967

Nursie, our English nanny, with our golden labrador, Prince, at
Zapallar Beach, Chile, circa 1969

President Johnson and Papa in the Oval Office, circa 1969. Papa's sofa chair ensured he sat lower than LBJ.

Nursie on the Imperatore Yacht (Roy Cohn's old boat) Edgewater, NJ. The occasion was my first wedding, 1981.

Uncle Peter, my godfather (The Serene Highness Prince Peter Schoenburg-Hartenstein of Austria) at my first wedding, 1981

Chatting with Sen. John Glenn at a 1980's party in NYC hosted by my boss.

With my husband, Dixon, on our wedding day – Garden Valley,
Georgia – September 1995

On a café terrace in Trinidad, Cuba – May 1, 2014

Dr. Richard D'Amico – My first and only trusted doctor and surgeon

Dr. Joe Contreras – My wonderful pain relieving doctor

Dr. Deena Graham – The only oncologist to diagnose me
correctly and to care about me

CHAPTER EIGHT

FOR LOVE AND MONEY (NOT ALL AT ONCE)

My marriage to Johnny was a lot like our wedding: lots of fun, something always going on, but ultimately, a journey that didn't go anywhere.

Plus, I paid for everything.

Johnny and I were married in a Greek Orthodox church in Manhattan, and later that day we celebrated with a huge group of friends, cruising up and down the Hudson river on a yacht, the Imperatore. The yacht was formerly owned by Roy Cohn, a New York attorney who at the time was both famous and infamous as a power broker, headline maker, and man about town. We rented the Imperatore after Cohn had sold it, but the idea of floating around on Roy Cohn's yacht added to the sense of happy recklessness that marked the whole day. We wheeled around and around the harbor, the champagne flowed, and I was definitely happy.

All day, I avoided the glowering presence of Papa and Mummy, who came to "celebrate", but who couldn't help showing by their tight-faced politeness how little they thought of their new son-in-law. In fact, they distrusted Johnny from the start. At the time, I shrugged it off as classic Papa and Mummy behavior. Papa's assessment of my new husband, "He's a bullshit artist," rivaled the blunt and legendary CIA cables he became known for in Washington.

Still, much as I hated to concede the point to my parents, I knew what Papa meant, and somewhere inside of me I knew I was headed for trouble. But Johnny was so much fun.

The appealing thing about Johnny—besides his intense good looks—was that he came by his fun honestly. He never drank in his life, never smoked anything, and never did drugs. He truly loved life and seized it with both hands, just like I did. So, we had that in common. But his charm was soon outweighed by his flaws.

The first flaw to surface was his resentful competitiveness. For example, he taught me how to water ski, but the moment I became good at it—when people started saying, "Wow, she's good!"—he didn't want to water ski with me anymore. Even though he was a good water skier, he was terrified of being shown up and compared to anyone else, even his own wife.

After our marriage we moved into a condo that I paid for, but I put it in both of our names (another mistake). If I hoped for a permanent love nest, it cracked under the weight of more flaws. For one thing, he brought women back to our condo. Some of the time, it may have been a case of old fashioned man-woman cheating. Other times he expanded his reach by using the line that he was the nephew of Aristotle Onassis and ran a home business as a fashion photographer.

The worst moment was when I came home to find my "artistic" husband aiming a camera at six unrobed women laying on my bed.

He also had a short fuse that was constantly lit by our innocent new puppy, who happily chewed up the telephone cords and anything within inches of the floor. This sweet puppy had no idea he was upsetting the man of the house until Johnny started hitting him.

Then Johnny started hitting me. I figured out pretty quickly what was going on, and I thought, "Okay, so what are you trying to prove here, Deborah? Are you saying you want to have a miserable life, that you want to prove to yourself nobody loves you (because your father didn't), and that you should be badly treated like this?" I didn't need anybody to help me figure it out. No therapy required—that came later.

For me, the light burst through on a raw and freezing January day while I was in my pajamas, wheezing and woozy, and medicated from a bad lung infection. I wrapped a bathrobe around my pajamas and walked out with nothing but my shoes and car keys and drove straight to a friend's house.

According to my lawyers, leaving my home that day was the worst thing I could have done because, according to the law in New Jersey at that time, I had abandoned my property. That was infuriating, because I was the one who had paid for it.

So began what I'm told was one of the longest divorce proceedings in state history. I left Johnny in 1983, and we were not divorced until ten years later. Johnny changed attorneys six times and moved across the country to California. As for me, I didn't have any money (not anymore, anyway) but my attorney assured me his firm would take care of everything. We started ten years of slow-motion justice, which consisted of endless and expensive rounds of filings, depositions, and legal consults.

I was thirty-eight years old by the time divorce came through, and by then Johnny had won by attrition. In the final court proceeding, Judge Andrew Napolitano (who has since lucked out of the depressing life of a divorce court judge to become a TV pundit), ruled that I was doing well, while my ex was struggling.

Later, somebody told me that a few days before my divorce was finalized, Judge Napolitano was seen partying with a friend on

Johnny's boat. I also learned that the judge lived a few floors above me in the same building on Overlook Avenue in Hackensack, NJ.

Can you blame me for thinking he should have recused himself? Instead, Johnny got the condo. I got a used car.

****

Life went on. I never missed work; I didn't go into a funk. My character was to power through and not to ask for sympathy or help. As a child in Ethiopia, I fled to my caves where I learned the first lessons of self-reliance and the art of living a full life without the need for demonstrable affection. My father had walled off his love from me, and so did my first husband. However, the comparison ends there, because I have never stopped loving or admiring my father.

That's not to say I couldn't see a possible connection between my shaky choice of husband and the detached treatment I received from my father as a child. Of course, people made the leap that life as an ambassador's daughter had to be enviable, "Oh, how lucky you are to have such a wonderfully accomplished father!" They would have been amazed to think I had daddy issues when the truth was, if I poured out my heart (which I refused to do), I would have been at the head of the line. "Daddy issues? Are you kidding me? I'm the first one to say it!"

So, I had a lot to work through, but I did it alone. As a child, I had stabilized myself in the solitude of an Ethiopian cave. As a grownup, I searched for another cave and found one: my career. After my marriage ended, my career took off. I turned out to have a creative talent for marketing, problem solving, and running things. At the same time, I changed my whole life. I no longer needed to keep needy people around or loan them money, just to prove that the neglected child had turned into the Rock of Gibraltar. No, that part of my life was over.

A friend of Johnny's and mine (I'll call him Adam) was sympathetic to me during that time. In a divorce, friends get divided up like property, and Adam hired me to work for him. Together we created a start-up company that was a spinoff of his family business that had clients all over Manhattan. In our new business, Adam put me in charge of creating a computerized office directory for business lobbies—the modern answer to the stodgy, embossed company rosters seen on every lobby wall. This was a computer screen that allowed visitors to touch the first letters of a name, and the screen would scroll to the company they were searching for. For the time, this was cutting-edge.

After explaining the rough outlines of the idea, Adam shoved me out of the nest. "Now you've gotta figure it out, get it built, and then you're gotta sell it."

So I did. The joy of it all: I was good at it too. I even created a Mylar screen for the keypad, which was eye-catching and a great selling point. I would lug this 150-pound thing all over Manhattan on a trolley to show it off to potential customers, including commercial real estate developers, management firms, architects, and designers.

Adam and I created a business arrangement which gave me equity in the start-up company and a share of profits, and I ended up making sales all over the country. It wasn't quite like helping the rest of the world—this was no UNICEF—but at least I was out there, helping people problem-solve and create value for their businesses.

The day came when I sold a package to a company for two million dollars. According to our business arrangement, my share should have been $200,000. However, instead of money another life lesson was coming at me like a freight train—this one in the form of a worthless, six-figure check.

I should have known something was up when Adam asked me not to cash the check for a period of time. I was okay with that because he was paying me a good salary anyway. Little by little the truth came out—Adam's family business had, as they say, major tax problems, as I discovered when I came by the main office one day—only to be stopped by a padlocked door.

So, I was alone and out of work in New York City. But instead of being terrified the experience energized me. I had sprung myself from a bad marriage and gone on to create an innovative business concept and design that clients were willing to pay good money for. It proved to me I could do anything I wanted to. I didn't have to go to Harvard like my sister Alexandra, or to the University of Chicago, like my brother Ted; I had created my own successful life.

For years, I held on to that worthless six-figure check, seeing it as a symbol of defiant independence. In good times and bad, that check certified I was powering through life on my own. At some point, I lost the check during a move. But by then, I didn't need the symbolism anymore.

Before long, I had landed my next job with a healthcare company that runs a large network of nursing homes and similar care facilities. Jack, the owner, was a prominent businessman, real estate investor, and philanthropist. He had more energy and professional interests than ten men. He owned a private plane and houses in East Hampton (and other chi chi places), and he had a slew of commitments that needed looking after. That was my job. My role became to oversee all his daily investments, his plane, his staff, and all his residences, plus his budget and his social calendar. I was his assistant, social secretary, and chief of staff—all rolled into one.

Plus, Jack had important friends who required attention. This was not a problem for an ambassador's daughter who had grown up with the likes of a Nixon, Kennedy, Vanocur, and Ellington hanging out in the family living room. As Jack's assistant, I juggled the needs of the Gary Harts, the Bill Clintons, the many Kennedys (who seemed to be everywhere), and many more. I made sure to keep all their business records straight and billed their offices for the use of Jack's private plane.

Another of my responsibilities was arranging parties for Jack's business associates, a task which required more finesse and caused more headaches than one might think. Jack would invite his colleagues from Wall Street and one or two celebrities. I was in charge of pulling everything together, from picking the restaurant and the menu to organizing the entertainment and taking care of the celebrities.

One year, Jack invited both Senator John Glenn and Senator Ted Kennedy to the same party. When I saw the guest list I warned Jack, "They don't like each other," but he just shrugged it off. It was too late to change anyway. The two men arrived and were coolly polite to each other, just jovial enough not to arouse curiosity. But once the surface amenities were over, the two American icons peeled off into different parts of the room, each to create their own sphere of influence.

That night, I brought Senator Glenn a plate of food and sat down to chat for a moment. Instead, our conversation lasted forty-five minutes, ranging from what it was like to be in space, to all the whys and wherefores that had lured him into politics. He was a lovely man. ("Of course, you shared with him that you were an ambassador's daughter," somebody said to me much later. "Never!" I replied. My father had taught me to be curious about everything and everyone. The point was not to make other people curious about me.)

A funny thing; much later my husband, Dixon, happened to be sitting next to Senator Glenn on a flight, and they discovered they both had ties to Ohio—Glenn was a native son, and my husband went to Ohio State University—and they formed that fleeting bond that travelers often do and enjoyed a friendly half-hour chat together. Both my husband and I, in wildly different circumstances and different times, had found John Glenn to be a gracious, unassuming, and down-to-earth human being.

As for the Kennedys, they inhabit their own world and make their own rules.

At one party, Ted Kennedy arrived, and I dashed off to get him a drink. No sooner had I put the drink in his hands than the media burst in the room—cameras, reporters: the whole entourage—and Kennedy shoved the drink back at me so fast it spilled all over my dress. Of course, he didn't notice, or maybe he didn't care. The important thing was to keep the photographers from snapping a photo of him with a drink.

By then I was in my 30s and had spent my whole life observing the Kennedys from near and afar. As a child of seven, I had met tall, handsome John Kennedy in the Oval Office. He was a powerful president who made me laugh and was very kind, who gave my brother a tie clip and my father a fabulous job that opened up the world for me, especially the world of Ethiopia. As a young girl, I met Bobby Kennedy when he visited Ethiopia. My memory is of a man who was polite and dignified, but also charismatic, friendly, and interested—even in a little child like me.

Ted was another kind of Kennedy. From what I observed, his mission was to become the center of attention and enjoy each party to the full—with a full glass.

My father wrote in his memoirs about the drinking behavior of Ted Kennedy's staff during the days surrounding the funeral of the president. Because of the shock and horror of the assassination, many people were drinking heavily, and everyone was getting a pass for their unsteady behavior. That said, the Kennedy staffers took things too far. The night before the funeral, some of Kennedy's staff piled into an elevator, and one of the more drunken members started making racial slurs.

Unknown to the staff member, the other people in the elevator were Haile Selassie's son, the crown prince of Ethiopia, and other Ethiopian officials. Although it was late at night, the prince immediately called my father with an angry ultimatum: He told my father that unless Ted Kennedy apologized immediately, on the day of JFK's funeral the Washington Post was going to get a front-page story that would destroy the civil rights image of the Kennedys' forever. My father had a real diplomat's dilemma on his hands, but he met it head on. No such story ever appeared, and Ted's image was preserved.

It was rather funny, and peculiar, how the Kennedy clan kept reappearing in my life. At one of the parties I arranged, a Kennedy of the younger generation asked me to accompany her to the bathroom where she opened up a large satchel and started removing the pictures from the walls. We were at Maxim's, one of New York's finest restaurants in the late 1980s, where even the bathroom art had value.

"Wait a minute—what are you doing?" I gasped. In reply, she ordered me to start helping her: "Do you know who I am? I'm (so-and-so) Kennedy."

And I said, "I don't care if you're a Kennedy or a busboy, this is outrageous," and I walked out. I don't think she was used to being talked to that way.

Later that night, the chief of staff to another Kennedy asked if I could join them at an after-party event. "Sorry, I said, "but I'm working, this is my job."

"No, no, we talked to Jack. This party is almost over. He said you could leave. We're headed over to Billy's Restaurant, and we'd like you to join us."

So, a bunch of us in the younger set piled into Jack's limo and headed for 42nd Street, where we picked up some additional guests from the street: women with big hair, dresses hiked up to crotch-level, and high heels like skyscrapers. Now, I like parties, but I was never gladder to get home from a party than I was that night.

The next morning, I was at my desk when my phone rang. The caller identified himself with these horrifying words: "I'm a re-porter with the Boston Globe." He proceeded to recite exact details from the whole raucous, Kennedy-centered evening, and ended with the chilling question: "Do you have a comment?"

I began to gasp out a litany of denials when the guy burst out laughing—it was Jack's driver, enjoying a little after-hours humor.

****

So, that was my world in the 1980s.

I was in my 30s—that wonderful, can-do-no-wrong decade of life when you're old enough to have experience and skills, and young enough to enjoy them, along with everything else life has to offer. I was proving to myself I could make my way in life without benefit of close family, and my career was in high gear. Even though I was in the middle of an epic divorce proceeding I was still pretty satisfied with everything. That's when my personal life took an-other sharp turn.

I had joined a gym, not to socialize, but to do some serious work-outs. But every time I walked in or out, a guy named Rob made a point of saying hello, soon followed by, "How about having a cup of coffee with me?"

On such seemingly insignificant moments life can turn on a dime—or at least on the cost of a cup of coffee. Rob and I ended up together for ten years. We lived together for eight of those years, although I kept my apartment in Fort Lee, New Jersey the whole time. Maybe that personal space represented my escape route, an-other grownup cave where I could get away from the world and totally be myself.

Rob opened up a new dimension in life: he had two kids, a son and daughter, both under the age of ten. That made me happy be-cause I dearly wanted children, and I enjoyed them. My own child-hood was vivid in my mind, so I never felt that alienation many adults feel when a child enters their life; I understood kids, and I liked them.

Still, however much you may enjoy children (and they may en-joy you) blending that affection into a family doesn't always work. To this day, I am still close to Rob's son, but his daughter and I never got past the hard truth that I wasn't her mother, never would be her mother, and most importantly—wasn't worthy of being her mother.

Even small, daily moments like asking her to fill the dishwash-er were flashpoints for all-out war. "You're not my mother; I don't have to do that," or "Dad! She's making me vacuum the floor, and I don't have to, do I?" It was painful for all of us, and yet to our credit, we made it work for a long time.

Rob was a lovely guy, a hard worker who never went to college, but he had a good job in the steel fabrication business. He didn't have that Ivy League aura that I figured would impress my parents, but funny thing, they really liked him. He wasn't a smooth talker like Johnny, and his accent had a rough New Jersey edge to it, but he was genuine. To their credit, my parents picked up on that.

Rob had asked to meet my parents, which was another upfront, straightforward thing about him that was impressive. We had gone to Europe for a vacation and my parents (who changed domiciles like some people change shoes) were living in Puilly, right outside of Geneva, Switzerland. So, we worked out a visit and ended up staying two nights with them. The greatest compliment my parents could have paid to our relationship was the fact that afterwards my mother would regularly write to me, "Well, are you married yet?" And I would say, "I'm not interested in getting married." And she would reply, "Well, I hope you're going to get married, because you're wasting your time raising someone else's two children if you ever want to settle down to have your own!"

Marriage was not to be, and even an onslaught from my mother and various friends couldn't change that. As they predicted, Rob did well in life, and today probably even qualifies for the top 1%. Yes, he could have taken care of me in high style, and he wanted to. "But I don't want anyone to take care of me," I argued then, as now. "I want to work; I want to build my own life!" At the time, I hadn't proved myself yet, but I was eager to show I could become successful on my own.

More fundamentally, Rob had a way of expressing insecurities in a way that grated on me. He always had to be right, to be smarter, to know more. For example, we would be talking in private, and I would express an opinion that he didn't agree with. But later, when we were with other people, he would use my words and opinions as if they were his own. I had grown up in a world where people confidently expressed their own ideas and opinions, and it was assumed that different points of view would range across the spectrum. People who had to borrow their opinions from someone else didn't impress me. In a relationship, small, intermittent annoyances like these are like a pebble in a shoe—at some point they become intolerable.

People thought I was crazy to give Rob up, but I was restless in a way I couldn't explain—except that I knew I was meant to keep moving on.

****

I met Dixon in November of 1994 at a weekend football party in New Jersey. It was a big group of casual friends getting together for chili and burgers and beer. Dixon was a southern boy (born in Georgia) and an entrepreneur who co-owned a food contracting business. As far as I was concerned, he was simply one of the guys at the party. He struck me as pretty shy and living in his own world. So, I was pretty surprised when at one of the parties he said to me, "Listen, I have two tickets to go to see the Cowboys-Giants game at Giants Stadium on Christmas Eve. Would you like to go with me?"

Not bothering to disguise the shrug in my voice, I replied, "Sure, why not?"

That game in 1994 was apparently one of the first NFL games to be televised on Christmas Eve, but the rarity of the event was lost on me. Soon after saying, "Sure," I thought, "Wait a minute, I'm not interested in this guy, I'm not interested in the Giants or the Cowboys, and sitting outside in the freezing cold is the last thing I want to do anytime—especially on Christmas Eve!"

I expressed my change of plans to Dixon as diplomatically as I could. He said, "Okay, that's fine, no problem. Merry Christmas. Talk to you later."

Later, I found out my future husband hated the idea of going to that football game for the same reasons I did, but somebody had given him tickets. He was just trying to find a reason to ask me out.

But from that rebuff on, the "quiet man" didn't give up. He came up with all sorts of reasons to ask me out. How about dinner with his best friend and his daughter? A birthday party? A Broadway play? I was running low on excuses.

Finally, on January 21, 1995, we went out on our first date. Barely nine months later, on Dixon's forty-seventh birthday, September 1, 1995, we were married.

This time I didn't run away. This time I worked through things. I can't fully explain the alchemy I had with Dixon or why it didn't happen with the others. Dixon was—and is—a person who keeps to himself, who is remote and aloof. In the mysterious way we all have of pulling our past along with us, perhaps that aloofness reminded me of my father. Yet, Dixon also knew what he wanted, and he kept pursuing me even after being rebuffed. That showed a kind of determination and character that I admired.

In any case, another instinct was also at work—I dearly wanted children.

That issue came to a head two months after our first date. We were having breakfast in a neighborhood diner and suddenly Dixon said, "Deborah, I'd like to live with you the rest of my life." And I said, "What does that mean? Do you want to get married?" He looked at me a little confused (this was the '80s after all, and for a lot of people marriage was just one option among many). I forged on. "I've lived with someone, but I'm not into that anymore. I want to have children. So, I'm either going to get married and have children, or I'm going to have children alone, with a sperm donor."

I don't know if that amused him or something, but he said, with a kind of laugh, "Oh, no, no, no. I have nothing against getting married!"

Meanwhile, I'm thinking, "Wait a minute, I don't want to get married again; what the freaking hell am I saying?"

But from there, things fell into place as naturally as the change of seasons. It helped that Dixon never showed too much emotion (except for his beloved Ohio State Buckeyes), so planning was easy.

"Shall we get married by a justice of the peace?"

"Whatever you want to do."

"This year? Next year?"

Didn't matter; Dixon went with the flow.

"How do you feel about children?"

"That's fine with me," he said.

This guy was growing on me in a big, big way. "Why don't we get married in Georgia?" I said. "You talk so much about your family farm, and growing up there, and how it means so much to you. I don't have any place that means that much to me."

****

Five months before our wedding I turned forty years old—not exactly the ideal age for a woman to think about getting pregnant. My doctor estimated it would probably take me at least a year.

Well, so much for the myth of fertility declining with age! Our wedding plans weren't even on paper yet when one morning I jumped into bed with Dixon with some wonderful news:

"I'm pregnant!" I crowed, to which laid-back Dixon drawled, "I thought you said it was going to take you a year ... well, I guess up to a year?" Then we both started laughing. Pure happiness. And all those darting little questions that had been snapping at my mind about my age were put to rest. I was going to have a child!

As a person who had grown up without signs of affection, it was a sweet prospect to know I could look forward to getting affection from my children. I recalled how just weeks after our first date on Valentine's Day I got Dixon a gift, and he hadn't responded affectionately at all—and that was a red flag for me. I told him then, "If you're not capable of being affectionate, let me know now!"

"Oh, I'm just slow," Dixon said. His reply, backed up later by his actions, satisfied me. Still, the promise of a child was a fulfillment of the affection I was eager to give and to receive.

Today, I am astonished to think how starkly opposite my instincts were from my parents, and I wonder if it didn't represent a kind of strange, asymmetrical justice: Papa and Mummy had enormous affection only for each other, but very little for their children, while I planned to lavish all my affection on my children and could live—if necessary—with less affection from my husband.

As it turned out, life had other plans altogether, and delivered them in a pretty cruel way. I suffered a miscarriage every year, from my fortieth birthday on until I turned forty-five. That wonderful surprise pregnancy before the start of our married life? It was the first miscarriage of five, and those included two attempts to become pregnant using donor egg cycles, a different procedure than the more familiar in-vitro fertilization.

The first of those donor attempts brought such early happiness—I was pregnant for five months with twins. Everything seemed normal, until—suddenly, it was not. The next attempt was too brief to bring happiness. The second doctor told me (rather brutally, I thought) that the embryos "weren't very good", and he wasn't surprised they didn't "take." My disappointment and grief were overtaken by anger that he had gone ahead, even though he knew the attempt was headed for failure.

I so wanted children! While it was still possible to have our own children, Dixon had resisted the idea of adoption. I agreed, because it doesn't work unless both parents are eager to welcome an adopted child into the home. When I turned fifty, I said, "You know, I wish you would have let me adopt," and Dixon said, "If you still want to, now we can." But by then, my question was more wistful than realistic. I didn't want a child to be raised by "elderly" parents. Besides, at our age, it would have been difficult to pass the adoption requirements in our state.

Disappointment doesn't begin to describe the hollowed-out void of being childless. But Dixon and I made it through. We are each strong in our own right, and from the beginning we understood that about each other. He reminded me, "Had you been needy, I wouldn't have gone out with you to begin with." He saw a girl who was strong enough to take care of things on her own, and who didn't need a lot of reassurance from outside herself. We had an unspoken understanding of what we needed from each other, and I'm sure that's why I was able to handle the miscarriages, the endless doctor appointments—everything, on my own. Dixon's attitude was, "Look, I'm a decent guy, a very honest guy, and what you see is what you get. These are my interests and you have yours. You should know I love you and respect you."

And the upshot was, I'm glad we did not go forward to adopt, because I was about to face a very personal challenge: a long fight with cancer, and it would have been unfair to put a child through that.

In many ways, cancer was the highest cost of all for being the ambassador's daughter: my father had passed down the BRCA2 gene sequence, a genetic mutation for breast and ovarian cancer traced to Papa's Eastern European heritage.

Tests revealed that yes, I was a carrier of the BRCA gene. As I will explain in due time, it has impacted my life to its core.

Many years before my own crisis, Papa was hit with a life-altering blow of his own. Here's the difference: unlike my battle, which I kept secret for months even from close friends, my father's battle was carried out painfully in the glare of the media—and for all the public to see.

CHAPTER NINE

MY FATHER: "ENEMY OF THE ESTABLISHMENT"

One day in early spring 1978, I was living in New York and performing the sweet Sunday ritual of meandering over a late breakfast while reading The New York Times. When I happened to flip over to the back page, my stomach did a back flip: what I saw was a blaring magazine advertisement, accompanied by a huge photo of my father.

My heart began racing, so I remember the words in a disjointed way, but the essence of it was, "Edward M. Korry, US Ambassador to Chile: How to Ruin the American Man." Or words to that effect. The ad was touting a huge article in the upcoming March 1978 issue of Penthouse magazine.

In those days, serious public policy issues were given a platform in many publications, including the so-called men's magazines. This Penthouse article was especially hard hitting: My father, a former United States Ambassador for three presidents, was calling out the American government for betraying not only him—but for betraying the American people. The article, written by my father, was headlined: "The Sell-Out of Chile and the American Taxpayer". His opening lines set the stage for the disturbing true story. He wrote:

"For two years I have devoted my life to the lonely and futile struggle of trying to tell the American people what Jimmy Carter, like Richard Nixon before him, insists must remain top secret.

"My name has been on extreme-left assassination lists, my life has been threatened by the extreme right, my reputation has been shredded by ITT and CIA agents, and my bank account has been depleted, because I believe the electorate should hear the facts of a story that has dominated the media for the past four years—what the United States did in, and to, Chile."

I sat there devouring every one of the 5,000-plus words, rocked inside with an unexplainable mixture of sadness and pride. This was my father, in all his courage and fighting spirit. He wrote his article like the excellent reporter he had been, laying out in a clear, brutal, and direct way what he knew from his years as ambassador to Chile from 1967 to 1971.

True to form, he had never told us he had written this explosive article for Penthouse, or that the magazine intended to promote it in a huge, can't-miss-it advertisement in The New York Times. Like everything else Papa did, he and my mother operated alone, as if they had no children or family.

Papa pulled no punches. He promised to reveal "a network of under-the-table deals that would make Watergate look like a bedtime story." In detail, he described the political maneuverings of three presidents—his bosses, Kennedy, Johnson, and Nixon—and implicated the CIA and ITT (a.k.a. International Telephone & Telegraph—in that era the 1,000-pound gorilla among multinational corporations).

In his article, Papa was also nakedly frank about the dangers he faced for speaking out. He quoted the warning of a good friend, Ralph Dungan, his predecessor as ambassador to Chile. He wrote in the article that Dungan tried to discourage him from speaking out and quoted him as saying: "Don't try to put that stuff on record. Don't try to take on those guys. They can murder you."

Murder? Well, there are different kinds of murder. When I was a teenager, ragtag thugs had stormed our personal home in Santiago and sprayed bullets at the front gate. They would have murdered us all if it had been convenient to do so. In fact, the Chilean government considered the danger credible enough to offer Papa extra security. My father had bravely turned it down, because he said he refused to have us cowering every day behind guards and guns.

"If people want to kill you," he said, "guards and guns won't stop them."

As it turned out, other kinds of thugs (in better-looking clothes) were waiting for him in Washington and New York. The political establishment was ganging up to kill my father's reputation. It was planning to make him the scapegoat for the botched attempt to overthrow President Allende of Chile, the Marxist who had been duly elected president in 1971.

The charge against my father was bogus. In fact, it was directly the opposite of his express warnings to the power elite in Washington.

As he wrote in his article, my father was appalled to arrive in Chile in 1967 to see how deeply the United States had become enmeshed in Chilean politics. The US was taking responsibility for every facet of Chilean life, and he warned that this "incestuous relationship" was hurting both countries. Instead, my father advised that the United States should "disengage, quietly and prudently" and begin to introduce a low-profile policy throughout Latin America.

Despite his wise counsel, in 1971 forces at the State Department, CIA, and beyond—had taken meddling in Chilean politics to the ultimate degree, by orchestrating a coup to overthrow Allende. When it failed, Ambassador Korry was set up to take the fall for the failed Allende coup and the ultimate destabilization of Chile.

Then, the lie was reinforced by the destructively ambitious writer Seymour Hersh, who "mugged" my father on the front page of The New York Times.

My father, a former journalist whose own reporting was impeccable, bitterly regretted trusting Hersh. He had cooperated with Hersh on previous articles, but now Hersh was relying on sources at the CIA and State Department, who wanted to set up my father to cover-up their own complicity in destabilizing Chile.

Six years later, in an extraordinary turnaround, long after the damage was done, The New York Times published a retraction to clear my father's name. Known as the "2,300-word correction", it's the longest correction in the newspaper's history. It pretty much stands as the longest correction in any publication anywhere.

However, as the saying goes, you cannot unring a bell. For my father, and for my devastated mother, the effects of those lies echoed on and on.

****

As with most disasters, the moments before everything fell apart were completely ordinary. I was living in Briarcliff Manor, NY at my parents' home, when in 1975, my father was asked to testify before a Senate committee investigating the involvement of CIA and FBI in covert operations worldwide, especially in Chile. Of course, he would testify, he said. He had been ambassador in Chile, and he had nothing to hide.

However, my father was already sensing personal danger. In the Penthouse article he wrote: "My conversion from friend and employee to enemy of the establishment began early in 1975." As the Senate hearings were getting underway, "I alerted the Justice Department that I saw myself as a possible victim of CIA and ITT perjuries and conspiracies. I intended to clear my name but also show how our political system actually works."

As usual, Papa had made meticulous preparations to testify. He made trips to Washington, Chicago, and even to Paris, to interview old colleagues who had worked with him in Chile. He interviewed advisors to Henry Kissinger, State Department specialists, and his successor, the new ambassador to Chile.

During that period, despite the dangers he sensed, Papa must have been in his element. He was not only serving his country, but he was using his journalistic and investigative skills to uncover the truth about America's true involvement in Chile. The accusation of United States meddling and cover-up in Chile by the CIA and multinational corporations had been circulating for years, but after the Watergate cover-up and Nixon's resignation they came to the fore. Everybody sensed that the government (namely, the CIA) was involved.

Ironically, my father, who had served the country loyally and relied on the State Department and CIA for support throughout his diplomatic missions, also believed that corrupt forces within the American government were at work.

To re-read Papa's account today is unsettling, because he seemed to have almost an eerie sense of prophetic doom about the true nature of government in America. In the Penthouse article forty years ago, my father was really describing the operations of what in the twenty-first century is often called the deep state: a powerful latticework of government that operates in the shadows. It consists of elitists from every political party, or none at all, who have no allegiance to anything except their own self-interest.

Here's how my father explained it, four decades ago: "The tale of the United States in Chile would reveal how our political system has been converted into an insider's monopoly for the accumulation of power, wealth, and status."

He wrote that journalism had taught him that reality, like respectability, is not always what it seems.

Instead, he wrote, the concept of reality—at least in the corridors of power—is "a perverse maze of mirrors in which servants are transformed into masters, dwarfs into giants, and villains into heroes."

His article laid out, in detail, how the government had twisted reality to make him the villain.

****

As I read on, I was staggered to learn in detail the enormous pressures Papa had faced while our family lived in Chile. I was a teenager at the time, immersed in school and my own world, and my parents' lives were remote from my own. I accepted Papa was doing important work, but I had no way to grasp the complexities of his mission.

In fact, Papa went to work every day confronting, on one side, what he called the perverse maze of mirrors from Washington. On the other side, he faced the escalating fight in Chile between western capitalism and revolutionary Marxism. The prize was Chile itself, considered to be the crown jewel of democracy in Latin America.

The politics involved in holding Chile together—just from the American side—was complex.

In the early 1960s, the Kennedy administration was alarmed that prosperous Chile was growing vulnerable to the Marxist forces led by Salvador Allende. So, the White House began working behind the scenes to strengthen the already popular incumbent president Eduardo Frei. The Christian Democrat was seen as the best hope for free, western-style capitalism in Chile.

After JFK was assassinated in late 1963, President Lyndon Johnson continued that pro-Frei policy, and when my father was appointed ambassador in 1967, his task was spelled out clearly. Papa wrote, "The Johnson administration sent me to Chile with specific instructions to keep Allende out of power."

As noted earlier, my father had offended the touchy LBJ by turning down some high-level positions in his administration, but at the same time, President Johnson appreciated my father's judgment on international matters. But given the enormous problems growing in Chile at the time, Papa's appointment as ambassador in 1967 was probably LBJ's curse as much as it was a blessing.

Everything changed again when Richard Nixon took office in 1969.

Nixon and my father had had a good relationship ever since the future president visited Ethiopia back in the mid-60s, and Nixon was known to appreciate my father for always "telling it like it is". But shortly after taking office, Nixon abruptly fired my father.

Apparently, Ed Korry was tainted as ambassador to Chile not only because he had served two Democratic administrations, but because he was closely associated with Kennedy and Johnson's support of Eduardo Frei.

There was another possible reason for Nixon's anger. Oddly enough, it involved me.

One day, my father came home very upset. He sat me down, shook his finger at me, and said, "I told you not to state a word to anyone, at any time, about presidential candidates, or give your opinion about who you would vote for. I told you that if you did it would reflect on me. But you did it anyway, and now I'm probably going to pay for it by losing my job!"

I was stunned. I had done nothing of the kind! I asked what

he was talking about. He said one my classmates had gone home and reported that we had a mock vote at our school and "Deborah Korry voted for Humphrey." This was taken to mean my father was a supporter of Hubert Humphrey, Nixon's presidential rival. I protested I had never said a word to anyone about any presidential race.

More to the point, there never was a mock vote at school to begin with!

Besides, I told Papa, I had no idea who he supported in the presidential race.

My protests didn't matter. Papa believed what he heard. In addition to my supposedly uncontrollable nature, he and my mother now believed I was responsible for tainting Papa's standing with the president. This went to the top of the list of my transgressions and became one of the main reasons he and Mummy wouldn't speak to me—and, in fact, ignored me—for more than a year.

In fact, there was no end of political mischief-making that may have led to my father's firing. Another theory was that a vengeful Nixon wanted to sweep away all of the Kennedy influence in Chile, which was the attempt to solidify a permanent, western capitalist government in Chile. It would be, in effect, Camelot's alternative to Cuba. As the appointee of Kennedy and Johnson, my father could be viewed as part of the Camelot camp.

Well, if Papa's firing was Nixon's petty attempt to destroy Camelot, it didn't work. The State Department stepped in to urge Nixon to back down and rehire my father—which he did.

Ironically, when Nixon reappointed my father as ambassador to Chile, that set the stage for the ruination of my father's life and his reputation.

What would have happened, I wondered, if Papa had said "No!" when Nixon asked him to come back? Instead, he was sent back to

Chile, where powerful forces in Washington had set the stage for making him the scapegoat for the Allende mess.

****

Fast forward to 1976, when the Senate hearings began.

I was taking the two-year Katharine Gibbs program for college women in New York City and living in Briarcliff NY at my parents' home. Our relationship was operating in the usual polite and distant way that had been familiar to me since my childhood. Yet, as the political heat rose, everything became profoundly different.

My parents, sensing the political danger facing Papa, went into high gear. They began contacting people in government, the media, and in the diplomatic corps—in all the worlds that my father had operated in for more than a quarter of a century. On one hand, they needed to be updated on the net that was tightening around my father; on the other hand, they were reaching out to people to help, believe, and listen to him. Papa was not getting any official briefings, so he couldn't understand why the government he had served for so long, and so well, was trying to destroy him.

What's more, as a former journalist who prided himself on objectivity, he could not understand why the media was allowing his reputation to be so unjustly smeared. All he could think about was getting his name cleared.

My mother was completely preoccupied with helping him, writing letters, and contacting old and influential friends ... but most of their friends had no stomach for standing by him in foul weather.

During this time, although we were living in the same house, the only attention they paid to me had an edge to it. My mother alternated between treating me with grim silence, to turning on me in a fury with stinging words: "Do you have any idea what your father is going through?" as if, somehow, I was the culprit.

They always lived as if it was just the two of them. That didn't change. The difference was, now it really was just the two of them.

****

The Senate hearings had been a trap. My father was given only two hurried, twelve-minute sessions to give his testimony. The official storyline being developed was the exact opposite of the truth: my father was being maneuvered into the position of having personally orchestrated the failed coup against Allende.

To make things worse, as my father began to protest his treatment, the powers-that-be used his protests as proof he was guilty. Papa wrote, "Reporters were being told by some people in ITT and the CIA, and by some senators, that I was a perjurer who was now off my rocker."

My father kept fighting back, and eventually he made enough noise that 60 Minutes did a feature segment and interview with him and my mother on January 9, 1977, entitled "The Korry File".

Nearly a quarter of a century would pass before my father was featured on 60 Minutes again.

After his years of faithful service to America, my father was now being branded as a liar who had gone insane. Everything my father fought for, believed in, and dedicated his life to, was disintegrating, piece by piece, by the very government he had tried to serve.

But to make Papa's disgrace stick in people's minds, the lies still needed to be written within a dazzling, unforgettable storyline. That was supplied by a brash New York Times reporter named Seymour Hersh.

****

My father knew Hersh. Everybody in government knew Hersh. He had a monster-sized ego that was further bloated by winning the Pulitzer Prize for his Vietnam reporting. Hersh was a frenetic, nervous-acting guy who never completed a sentence. Because of his feverish, hyperactive manner he was famously described like "a dandelion blowing in a windstorm". Yet he was also the golden boy of The New York Times, because he got big, award-winning stories.

Hersh didn't set out to specifically ruin my father; his fault lay in listening to government sources that were feeding him false stories, which implicated my father in plots to overthrow Allende. For Hersh, the real prize in the Chile story was incriminating Secretary of State Henry Kissinger to bring about his downfall. So, Hersh put together a pact from the devil and approached my father. "I need your help in getting Kissinger. If you don't help me, I will nail you."

This account came from my mother and brother, as told to author Robert Miraldi, who wrote a book about Hersh titled Scoop Artist. My father was outraged at Hersh and refused to cooperate. He complained to his friends at The New York Times, but nothing happened.

So, Hersh wrote his big article. In it, he even charged my father with lying to Congress in his Senate testimony. Now the story had real legs: According to Hersh's reporting, my father would stop at nothing to keep Allende out of office, and to get it done he used his influence as ambassador and even colluded with the multinational giant ITT to disrupt the Chilean election process. Hersh portrayed my father as a cloak-and-dagger figure who had worked behind the scenes to accomplish his ends.

My father was in anguish. He called out to his good friends at The New York Times to

appeal to the publisher, Abe Rosenthal, another friend of my father's, to set the record straight. Papa reached out especially to his good friend Dick Witkin, the transportation reporter and my father's colleague way back in the day when they were young reporters together in Europe.

Nobody, not even Dick Witkin, wanted to intervene. In near despair, my father would cry out, "Why isn't Dick doing something about this? Why won't anyone help to correct the record?" But none of his colleagues or friends at The Times would step forward to help him.

In 1978, he was able to hit back hard in the Penthouse article, but the impact was immediately blunted and absorbed by Washington's power elite. They merely closed ranks and froze him out.

He had been completely betrayed by America.

****

My parents lost everything. For a long time, my father couldn't even get a job. He had never concentrated on accumulating wealth, and my parents always spent what they had on maintaining the good life: travel in Europe, fine wines, and a beautiful home in Stonington, Connecticut—it all vanished.

One of the most painful things for him was the fact he could not provide for my beautiful, socialite mother in the manner to which she had been accustomed. In a galling turn of events, my once-powerful diplomat father, ambassador to two countries, was reduced to asking for financial help from my sister Alexandra, who by then was a successful lawyer. Not only was asking for help from a daughter embarrassing and painful, it did nothing to salve the wounds of hardship. My mother was a big spender, and she continued to feel she was entitled to a diplomat's lifestyle, so my father had the constant worry of having to maintain appearances.

My mother never got over the collapse of their way of life. However, true to form, she and my father continued to inhabit their own universe of two, relying on my sister financially to maintain their lifestyle without showing a care in the world—and without expending any time to be with Alexandra or their grandchildren.

Then, during their years in Briarcliff Manor, NY and Stonington, CT, my father began to rally professionally. He gained jobs in academia and public service, but they were modest by the standards of his diplomatic years. Into the 1980s, the past continued to haunt him, until he finally took action.

"I feel like a man without a country," Papa said. "I want to pack up and get out of here." So, in 1985, they did. Papa and Mummy moved to Switzerland, where they lived on borrowed money, and Papa tried his hand at playing the market and writing a book. In time, both ventures faded.

Seven years later their funds were dry, and my father needed hip surgery. Even though the hip prosthesis he needed was made in Switzerland, he didn't have the $10,000 to stay there to have the procedure done. In 1992, they moved back to the US to have the surgery paid for by Medicare.

After years of anguish, feeling like people without a country, my parents settled down for good in North Carolina.

My father took up cooking. Before that, he had never boiled an egg.

****

It took seven years for the truth about my father to even begin to overtake the lies. Here's how it came about.

First, Seymour Hersh surfaced again. In 1981, the man who had helped to ruin Papa's reputation some five years before actually had the chutzpah to approach my father and ask for his help on another book! Hersh was still obsessed with Henry Kissinger, and he figured my father could help with some background information. He called up to ask to visit my parents, then living in Connecticut.

"You've got some nerve!" my father shouted into the phone. "You're asking me to do you a favor after that garbage you put on the front page of The New York Times?"

For the first time in a long time, my father held the cards. "If you want to talk to me," he told Hersh, "first you need to write a retraction of those lies and get it back on the front page of The Times!"

Well, Hersh had left The Times by then, but he did what Papa demanded—he got the so-called "2,300-word correction" on the front page of his old newspaper. Executive editor Abe Rosenthal was finally willing to do the right thing. Cleverly though, nowhere in the article did Hersh take any blame for contributing to the smear of my father. In fact, it wasn't even spelled out that he had written the first article. Very carefully, Hersh wrote, "Evidence has come to light suggesting that Korry was 'frozen out' of the White House, planning for the Allende coup."

True to his word, after the famous correction appeared, my father answered Hersh's questions about Henry Kissinger. And to his credit, later Hersh began to take grudging responsibility for his bad reporting and admitted, "I led the way to trashing him."

After the correction appeared, Papa was interviewed by the rival media outlet, Time Magazine (that was surely gloating). Papa took the high road, saying, "I've always believed in justice. But there was misreporting by The Times, and certain people knew that."

Papa also told Time Magazine that he had spent the past seven years "in a kind of isolation ward". But no—he wasn't bitter.

As for the "2,300-word correction?"

"It's a start."

****

Papa was right—it was a start. Eventually more and more stories began to be written about my father's ordeal. Then, almost twenty-five years after it all began, on September 9, 2001, my father was featured on another 60 Minutes segment about the smear campaign that had effectively ruined his life.

The story about Papa's ordeal at the hands of government probably would have gained strength after that night's telecast. Old colleagues and friends who had abandoned him may have started to come forward to make amends. That's what should have happened anyway—if history hadn't made a terrible turn just forty-eight hours later with the terror attacks of 9/11.

Suddenly, diplomatic grievances from a quarter of a century before didn't seem so relevant anymore.

****

Sometimes, when I would walk into Papa and Mummy's last home in North Carolina, I would see my father at the stove, stirring his favorite mixture of goulash and potatoes in a pot, and my heart would break a little to think about his fabulous life as a journalist, an ambassador, and a man who—in no small way—helped direct the course of history. Now, he was standing at a kitchen stove, stirring something in a pot.

Then again, for Papa, cooking felt right. Perhaps cooking was a way to restore his strong sense of order and justice. After all, when the cook brings all the ingredients together in a skillful and orderly way, the result is satisfying—even life sustaining.

I like to think that, for Papa, cooking was the farthest thing away from the disorder, confusion, and lies of politics. Cooking was wholesome and straightforward. It was the opposite of living in a perverse maze of mirrors where nothing—and no one—could be trusted.

CHAPTER TEN

CANCER

On July 27, 2008, I met a good friend for dinner at a cozy food and wine restaurant near my home in New Jersey. I had a lot on my mind and felt more than entitled to a nice evening.

As I walked in, Nancy looked up with a big smile, but it collapsed quickly into a look of shock and concern.

"Why do you have blood on your t-shirt?" she said.

"I do?" I looked down and sure enough, there was a dark red stain around my left breast.

I didn't plan to break my news in such a dramatic and vivid way, but looking back, maybe there was something fitting about it. In many ways, I am still the girl who pondered life in an Ethiopian cave, came to womanhood at the age of eight, and bolted from husband-number-one in a driving snowstorm. Like my father, I don't live life in a tiny script or in a supporting role. No matter what each day holds, I live it to the full, stage center.

"I have breast cancer," I said. Rather than wait for Nancy to look horrified, I plunged on. "I've just been to the hospital, and in a few days, I'm going back to have a double mastectomy. I suppose the blood is because I've just had my breasts poked with a medieval torture instrument, and I'm told there's more to come. They want to know if the cancer has spread to the other breast."

153

One of the best things about being with a trusted friend is that you know what she wants to know even before she asks.

"So, you want to know why I've decided to have a double mastectomy when I don't have to? The answer is, I'm sick and tired of what I have to go through every year. I go in for a mammogram, and because I have unusually cystic breasts, they have to do an ultrasound. Then they do an aspiration, and then there's this thing called a mammotone, where you're hanging over a table with your breasts flapping in the wind while they do more poking and pinching. It takes four hours, and sometimes I have to come back. I don't want to go through that stuff anymore. Besides, I don't consider breasts the hallmark of female sexuality. I've never thought that's what makes any woman, including me, attractive or sexy."

Nancy looked at me for a long moment. I knew she was shocked, but I was also grateful for her silence. She didn't offer that fluttering, female, "When can I bring over soup?" response I have never managed myself, and I don't expect it from anyone else either.

Then Nancy said, "I've never met anyone like you in my life. I can't believe how calm you are. You drop news on me like this, and you might as well have said you were changing your lawn care service. It's like you've already got everything figured out, and it's going to be okay. You are the most positive person I've ever met!"

Well, it's true. From the beginning of my diagnosis, I considered cancer an inconvenience rather than a catastrophe. Even now, after my cancer fight has gone from a quick knockout to a fifteen-rounder, I look at it as a challenge I simply have to power through.

There was an irony to my illness too. After a lifetime of polite alienation from the father I adored, I learned I could not escape one intimate connection with him. Thanks to genetic research I learned that I carry the BRCA gene—the cancer gene—traced to

Papa's eastern European Jewish heritage. Research shows that Ashkenazi Jewish women (meaning from Eastern European origin) are ten times more likely to have the BRCA1 or BRCA2 gene mutation than the general population.

Long before this became personal to me, the BRCA mutation was already getting a lot of publicity in the 2000s, thanks to advances in genetic research. The media began featuring many stories about women who were anguished to learn they had the mutation—and therefore a heightened risk for breast cancer.

As for me (another irony), when I was diagnosed with cancer, it never occurred to me to wonder whether I had a BRCA connection; I wasn't a person who worried about things like that. Only later did it become a central factor in facing cancer.

A few days after my dinner with Nancy, and the day before my surgery, I reported for my second round of medieval torture. A huge horse-sized needle, filled with dye, was stabbed right into my nipple—not once, but three times. The dye illuminated the lymph nodes so that, during the breast removal, the surgeon could check the nodes for cancer. No numbing, no anesthesia. It was the most excruciatingly painful thing I've ever been through.

After a few hours, the medical establishment got its pound of flesh (pounded flesh, was more like it), and I was free to go—for the time being anyway. I got dressed in a haze of half-dizzy nausea that I willed myself to shake off. I had things to do.

That night, less than twenty-four hours before my surgery, I went to listen to my friend Lidya sing in a concert at an outdoor park.

****

Now, I will begin at the beginning, with a caveat: Persons who get cancer often call it a journey, and at first, I was inclined to do the same. After all, journeys have beginnings and ends, they are often arduous, and they are filled with surprises—and that certainly describes dealing with cancer. Then I received a card from my sister Alexandra. The card's message said, "I promise never to refer to your illness as a journey unless someone takes you on a cruise."

I got a kick out of that. No sugary sentiments allowed here.

That's why I refuse to call cancer a journey. Instead, I offer my cancer experience in the hope it may, in some way, help others, mostly by urging them to keep fighting and keep questioning. Don't blindly accept what a physician may tell you. Keep exercising your own judgment. Disturbing as it may seem, accept the fact that some experts in the healthcare industry are more informed and up-to-date on the latest research than others, so never totally relinquish your responsibility to your own body.

My message is to stand up for yourself and don't let cancer, or the healthcare industry, intimidate you. Show you're involved in your own care, be proactive, and do your own research because—if your experience is anything like mine—you will need to.

****

It all began very simply. One day in July 2008, I felt a lump in my left breast. Should I worry? I just had a mammogram two months ago. It can't be cancer. Can it?

I'm not the kind of person who gets panicked or stressed; this was simply something I knew should be checked out. After work, I got a quick appointment with my gynecologist, a caring old-school physician who has seen me through multiple miscarriages and a variety of common female miseries.

Dr. Harvey Friedman confirmed through ultrasound that I did indeed have a lump in my left breast. He gave me the necessary prescription for a biopsy at Englewood Hospital in New Jersey.

The appointment was quick, scheduled for the very next day. At the time it didn't occur to me to be grateful. (In the years to follow, I would consider a next-day appointment the equivalent of winning the lottery.)

The pathologist, a very nice Russian man, explained the procedure: a needle would be inserted into the lump and cells withdrawn. Within ten minutes, he could determine if it was cancer.

Ten minutes? (Another brief fling with Lady Luck.)

Yes, it was cancer. The pathologist was direct and kind. He thought it was stage II, grade 3. "But we won't know until the tumor is removed and the pathology is done."

I didn't need his help getting to the ultimate step—I had already made up my mind that if it was cancer, I would have both breasts removed.

"So, what do I need to do next?" I asked.

"You need to meet with a surgeon and also a plastic surgeon," he replied.

I was still new at this cancer game, but now I could not stop. It was seven p.m. the day of the diagnosis, and it seemed completely reasonable to go out into a pounding rain to find a plastic surgeon.

I even had one in mind—not that he knew I was coming. I had heard of Dr. Richard D'Amico. He was—as they say—world renowned, and known to donate his time to help suffering people around the world. For me, a child of Ethiopia and a loyalist forever to UNICEF, his background appealed to me very much. Besides, he had a great reputation as a skilled plastic surgeon, and his office was just a few blocks from the hospital. That was all good enough for me.

Why I thought he would be there at seven p.m. on a gloomy night of pounding rain and shattering thunder I don't know, except that I was on a mission. I wanted to find out right away what was involved with removing my breasts and how quickly I could get an operation scheduled.

To my surprise, Dr. D'Amico's office was lit up and open. I walked in, all steamy and out of breath from the rain, and right into an empty waiting room. It had the melancholy look of a shop that was closing up for the night. I was aware I had to sell myself pretty quickly to the receptionist. "I don't have an appointment," I said, "but is there any chance I could see Dr. D'Amico? I just found out I have breast cancer."

Why did the receptionist respond so well to me? Maybe because I presented myself in a positive way. I was engaged in the process— even eager? I did not come off as an abject and defeated sufferer. I would come to understand that patients who act defeated, end up defeating their own cause. They make it difficult for a medical team to offer its best. Anyway, I think my eagerness touched something in the receptionist, because she looked at me with interest.

"He's just back from a medical mission to Africa, and his last patient has just left," she said. "But I'll see what I can do."

No more than two minutes later, I was with Dr. D'Amico, explaining my history, my physician care, and my need for his services. I told him I already knew I wanted to remove both breasts, and I was not interested in having a debate about it.

I could see he was startled. Without waiting for him to reply I went on, my voice steady and firm, "I know what I'm doing. For example, I already know that I have the same chance of getting cancer again whether you remove both breasts now or take out only a lump from one breast."

Dr. D'Amico looked at me with what I thought was heightened respect, and I knew it was because I was so direct and calm. No weeping, no fear, no drama.

"Okay, you know more than most people," he said. "Now explain to me—why we are removing both breasts?"

I explained as I had explained to Nancy—the endless mammograms, the aspirations, the mammotomes …

Dr. D'Amico actually listened to me. (Another rare and fleeting gift from the Hippocratic gods.) He said he respected my reasoning, and that it made sense. He and a breast surgeon would work together—the breast surgeon would remove my breasts and check my nodes for cancer. Meanwhile, Dr. D'Amico would be standing by to start the reconstruction process before I was even stitched up.

Right away, I trusted him. By the time I left his office, Dr. D'Amico had suggested an excellent breast surgeon and said he would call him personally to make sure I got an appointment, ASAP.

The appointment (with physician I'll call Dr. Barry S.) was scheduled without a hitch for the following day. (My dalliance with Lady Luck was holding). When I arrived, the waiting room was filled with people, most of them groups of two. One of them was sick; the other was there for support. Mothers and daughters, wives and husbands, sons and mothers—all somber faced and looking drawn and anxious. Everyone was there because of cancer.

I came alone. (A child of the Ethiopian caves knows her strength. She can do this.)

My name was called, and my short, contentious relationship with Dr. Barry S. began.

I was in the middle of explaining why I wanted both breasts removed when he interrupted me in that brusque, "I know what's best, end of discussion" tone that would become very familiar.

"You don't need to remove your breasts; all you need is a lumpectomy," he said.

Now it was my turn to interrupt him. "You don't need to waste your time explaining other options to me. You have a waiting room filled with people who look like they need a lot of hand-holding. Well, I don't. I just want you to explain what's involved with removing and reconstructing my breasts."

Dr. Barry S. huffed and struggled to maintain his dominance. Even after giving way he acted resentful, like a spoiled kid who just lost a softball game. He explained that even if I have both breasts removed, I'd need an MRI first, to make sure the cancer hasn't spread to the other breast.

"Okay, let's get going," I said.

****

My first surgery went well. The cancer hadn't spread to my nodes, and it was totally confined to my left breast.

As for Dr. D'Amico's breast reconstruction? Nothing less than miraculous. Both my breasts were gone, but it almost looked like they were still there.

"You can attribute that to your excellent pectoral development," Dr. D'Amico said, with a smile.

"Ah, so that's the payoff for being a work-out girl," I replied, smiling too. Dr. D'Amico explained that my muscular development allowed him to fill the area with more saline that usual. Again, lucky me. I was ahead of the game.

So far, my treatment had been straightforward and marked with good fortune. Then, just when I thought my journey was on the upswing, the cancer-treating industry threw up its first nasty roadblock.

To move forward with treatment, I needed pathology results

from Dr. Barry S. So far, I had gotten swift care, but after the promised seven-to-ten day wait for pathology results came and went, I started to wonder. I'm pretty relaxed when it comes to waiting for things, but I still thought it strange the surgeon hadn't even bothered to contact me since my surgery.

I waited three weeks before calling the office. The surgeon's business manager got on the phone and wasted no time putting me in my place.

"You and everyone else are looking for results!" she snapped. "He's on vacation. He'll contact you when he returns."

I had been raised in a diplomat's household, but I also knew when a little sour went further than sweet. "You shouldn't be in the medical field," I snapped back, "let alone be allowed to talk to a patient this way!"

A few hours later, I got a call from Dr. Barry S. who (surprise, surprise) was not on vacation at all. He was at home, and very upset that I would address his manager in such a way.

This experience, more than any other, made me determined to be my own best medical advocate. Little did I know how prevalent Dr. Barry S. and his manager's behavior is in today's cancer-treatment industry.

I finally received my pathology results, and in many ways, they were worth the wait. A further test, the Oncotype DX (I had grown fond of learning the names of all my procedures), revealed that because the cancer had not spread to my nodes, my odds of cancer coming back was just 11%. I was heartened. That meant there was an 89% chance that I would soon be cancer-free.

****

Maybe it was good I didn't know the truth all at once. It was still

2008 and today, nearly ten years later, I can sum up my overall experience with the healthcare profession in three words: "shocking medical care". To everyone who faces similar challenges, my message is that you must take charge of your own health and your own treatment. (If I had not taken charge of my health, I probably would not be here to write about it.)

Warning flags went up for me with my first oncologist, whom I'll call Dr. Francis F. I knew this wouldn't go well when he fumbled around for ten minutes, trying to access my file on his computer. He glanced at it for five seconds, then launched into a lecture about the progress of cancer treatment in the United States. Except for making some general recommendations, he had absolutely no insight or fresh information to offer about my case.

So, I went home and wrote him a letter, which concluded, "I thought I was seeing you to discuss my case and a treatment plan for me, not to discuss the history of cancer treatment over the past forty years. I also found it highly inappropriate that you would take three personal calls during the first fifteen minutes of my appointment."

I never got a response. A friend recommended a new oncologist. I'll call her Dr. Louise L. Her attitude (and file keeping) was better than Dr. Francis F.'s, but her recommendations were by-rote—straight out of a textbook. She recommended radiation and a drug called Arimidex, an aromatase inhibitor, which was considered appropriate treatment for my kind of cancer. However, I got no sense that she was adapting the treatment to my individual case.

That led to another realization: an oncologist's job is to make the cancer go away: period. Oncologists don't necessarily care—maybe it's better to say it's not their business to care—whether their treatments will cause other problems, say, to the lungs, heart, or vision. Radiation and chemotherapy are extremely harmful and toxic treatment options. Radiation therapy, especially, is like setting off dynamite to clean out the garage. Yet, this is still part of standard cancer treatment.

What's more, the data shows that half the patients who receive chemo and/or radiation probably don't need it. In fact, half of all breast cancers never reoccur, treatment or no treatment. The data is even more dramatic for my kind of cancer: estrogen-positive ductal and lobular invasive cancer. The data reveals that only 5% of the population with lobular invasive breast cancer benefit from chemotherapy. Yet, this is still the prescribed treatment for 99% of patients.

So, let's say the cancer is cured, but you develop heart disease, have a stroke, or some other major ailment that can be traced to radiation or chemo. By that time, it's not the oncologist's problem. Of course, highly skilled oncologists will look at the health and wellbeing of the whole patient. But experience forced me to reach a discouraging conclusion: that kind of oncologist is hard to find.

Bottom line: I would not radiate my body. After all, I had only a 11% chance of reoccurrence anyway. Why take the risk when my prognosis was so good?

As for Arimidex—okay. I did my research and realized that because my cancer was an estrogen-based cancer, it made sense to take a drug recommended for post-menopausal women.

I started taking Arimidex on October 31, 2008.

****

It was about this time that I decided to share the fact I had cancer with selected friends. I wasn't doing it for sympathy or attention, and—in fact—I had held off for a long time, not saying anything. I had the idea that by keeping it to myself, I could deal with the disease privately—in a quick businesslike fashion—and simply get on with loving life. This experience was tough enough without having to fend off the emotional reactions of friends and juggle people's well-meaning opinions about which doctor I should use and what treatment was best.

In the beginning, I didn't even tell my husband much except for the bare outlines of treatment. But as time went on, I wanted to be upfront with the important people in my life; it was a matter of being truthful and honest. I also had friends who went through cancer, and now that I had something of a track record of my own, it was a good time to share our experiences and insights.

One of the first friends to hear my cancer story was my good friend, Karen. She had been diagnosed with breast cancer in 2006, and despite opting for chemo and radiation she found out in 2013 that her cancer had metastasized. But she was holding her own, and I knew we could learn from each other.

Our conversation turned out to be life changing.

"Have you done genetic testing?" she asked.

"No. It's never occurred to me," I said.

"That surprises me," she replied, "because you say your father died of lung cancer, and you're Jewish on your father's side—Eastern European Jewish—which puts you right in the target area for the BRCA cancer gene."

"But I've already had a double mastectomy, so I've eliminated the BRCA problem without even thinking about it!"

"Not really," my friend replied. "The gene mutation also increases the risk for ovarian cancer, and that's much more difficult to treat."

We didn't even have to say it. We both knew ovarian cancer is the silent killer. By the time a patient gets symptoms, it is often too far advanced to cure. Despite promising advances in treatment, survival rates are still not good.

"I think you better go for genetic testing," Karen said.

I felt like a prisoner who was granted parole, only to hear the clang of the prison door again. Well, there was only one thing to do. I would get past this new obstacle and back to living.

Dr. Barry S., my surgeon, lived up to his track record as a difficult guy. I needed a referral to get insurance to pay for the BRCA genetic test, which cost $3,000 in 2008.

Dr. Barry S. refused to give me the referral. Instead, I got a scolding.

"You don't need a genetic test," he said. "You eliminated the risk when you had both breasts removed!"

Once again, it was up to me to educate him. I told him about the BRCA gene, my family background, and the heightened risk of ovarian cancer.

Grudgingly, Dr. Barry S. relented, and in the next few weeks I got the BCRA test. The results showed that, yes, Papa had passed on the BRCA gene to me.

Well, okay. This is good to know. Not a cause for tears or woe-is-me whining. Now I know. Let's get on with it.

Before the month was out, I was checked into Hackensack Hospital in New Jersey, and I was on the operating table of Dr. Daniel Smith. Like my plastic surgeon, Dr. D'Amico, this new doctor was a real find. He had an outstanding record as a surgeon and was one of the leading experts in a new technique called oophorectomy. I was only the fortieth or fiftieth person to have the procedure. The news made me feel rather jaunty and pioneerish, and it gave me some upbeat news to share with friends for a change. Besides, I liked Dr. Smith a lot. He listened, and he responded as one intelligent person to another. He got me. He started off by congratulating me on being so pro-active about my health.

"It's unusual for someone to forge ahead with genetic testing after surgery, after they think they have taken care of the problem," he told me, referring to my double mastectomy. "Your friend did you a great service by explaining the link between BRCA and ovarian cancer. You're lucky to know her."

I was lucky to know him, too. The surgery went well. Dr. Smith removed my ovaries and fallopian tubes, and all I had was a tiny scar in my belly button ... and just the very faintest, final farewell to the instruments of youth and motherhood.

****

The seasons passed. I continued to take Arimedex and other drug cocktails as prescribed. I had more follow ups (and clashes) with obtuse and disinterested physicians. I carefully scheduled my MRIs, juggled insurance claims, and pinched my skintight budget tighter (MRI's can cost up to $10,000 each).

One year, I skipped an MRI because insurance wouldn't pay for it, and my new oncologist (I call her Dr. Jill M.) didn't insist. Eight months later, I was in her office again.

"Why didn't you get an MRI?" she barked.

"I faxed and called three time to ask you whether I could skip that MRI since insurance had denied it," I replied as evenly as I could, trying to keep my temper. "I never got an answer, so I took that to mean we were in agreement—it wasn't absolutely necessary."

Of all the ways she could have replied ("Oh, I'm so sorry we miscommunicated ..." or, "From now on, let's agree to follow everything to the letter ....") Dr. Jill M. took the insulting route. "If you cared about your health, you would have gone and had it done regardless of whether the insurance covered it or not!"

Nice, caring, wonderful Dr. Jill M.! No, I would not be seeing her again. But healthwise, I was holding. All seemed well.

Then, in November 2014, I was lying in bed performing my regular self-breast examination when I felt a lump in my left breast. I didn't panic. I never panic. Besides, I had reason to believe it was simply scar tissue. I was determined to spend a happy holiday season and New Year, so I waited until early February 2015 to schedule an appointment to have the lump examined.

On the very day of my appointment, I felt another small lump outside of my breast, on my chest wall/axillary.

The results came from Dr. Rosalyn Stahl, a pathologist. I appreciated her approach because she was kind, thorough, and business-like: "The lump in your breast is cancer," she said briskly, "and the lump outside your breast is a cancerous node. So, let's talk about what we're going to do now."

I was calm. Since day one, I have treated cancer as an inconvenience. I have been blessed with a positive attitude that has carried me through every aspect of my life, every disappointment, every storm. I'm not having my legs cut off, or my vision taken away. I'm lucky!

Still, now that this was officially a recurring cancer, I was advised to have a series of other tests to ensure that the cancer hadn't metastasized (that is, spread to other parts of my body).

Like a hero in a play, enter again my skilled and highly-valued plastic surgeon, Dr. Richard D'Amico. By then, I'd had enough negative experiences to know I wasn't allowing anyone but him to do surgery on me. He did, and with such skill the aesthetics of my breast implants were never disturbed. A treasure of a man.

However, the new cancer has ramped up a new protocol of new

drugs, new oncologists, new everything. I had a new oncologist, whom I'll call Dr. Michael S. (oncologist #5), and by this time I was too cynical to mince words.

"I hope you can help me," I said, "because my experience with oncologists has not been good."

****

So, the year 2015 didn't start out as well as I hoped. Cancer was back and so were new doctors, drugs, consultations, and protocols. The good thing was the cancer was still localized in my breast area. The bad thing was, I still couldn't trust my physicians. That became clear when my latest oncologist, Dr. Michael S., asked me how my radiation treatments were going.

"What are you talking about? I never opted for radiation!"

When I expressed my frustration and discouragement, he suggested maybe I was depressed and should see a psychiatrist.

"I don't need a psychiatrist," I said, outraged, "What I need is an oncologist who actually reads my file before seeing me!"

Other doctors suggested other aggressive therapies, but I turned them all down. I was now diagnosed with recurring cancer (that is, local, regional cancer which had not metastasized). For that reason, I rejected the scorched-earth policy most doctors recommended. Radiation and chemotherapy amounts to killing the patient in order to cure the cancer.

For someone like me, who did not have metastasized cancer—and who thrived on living life to its fullest—my quality of life superseded poisoning my body.

Then in mid-October 2015, while visiting my mother in North Carolina, I felt a new lump in my left breast. By then, I was an expert. I knew it was cancer. I was just surprised the cancer had come back so quickly. It was just eight months since my last tumor was removed.

Before I decided to undergo surgery, I had a final run-in with Dr. Michael S. I simply didn't trust him. He hadn't read my files, and he knew so little about my case that I wondered if he had me mixed up with someone else. It was like he was on autopilot.

"How would you feel if it was you, your wife, or your children who were getting this kind of care?" I said.

"I thought you decided to do radiation and take the drug protocol," he said.

"If you had you looked at my file for twenty seconds, you would have known I hadn't!"

We both knew we would never see each other again.

"Good luck," he said.

****

I am a woman committed to defending my own health; I am intelligent, motivated, and willing and able to work with my physicians. Yet, most of the professionals I have met are uninvolved and unmotivated. I'm not an individual as much as I am "the next patient" in a long and annoying day. When I assert my rights as an individual—that I have a right to question my physician about my progress and a right to be involved in my own healthcare decisions—the responses careen from indifference to resentment to anger. But the effect is the same: most physicians refuse to listen to me. It's like being trapped in a dream where you are trying to communicate, and no sound comes out of your mouth.

One day, I was sharing my frustration with Karen, my friend with cancer. She looked at me with sympathy.

"They are all the same," she said.

At an unlikely moment, a ray of hope broke through. I had been scheduled for a round of infusions at Holy Name Hospital in Te-aneck, N.J. The day began like so many others: Report to the reception area. Sign in, sit back. Wait …. wait … wait for the next order from high command: "Report to cubicle 23."

I obeyed, but in my mind, I was like a resistance fighter, outwardly compliant, but inwardly fierce and ready to do battle. I went to cubicle 23, which in my mind had become "jail cell 23."

How much would patients' health be supported and even enhanced if we didn't need to fight the stress and weariness of waiting rooms, miscommunications, and indifference? I was mulling these things when, just then, a gentleman in a business suit passed in front of me and paused.

"Can I help you?" he asked.

What had he seen on my face? Did he see a soldier ready to do battle, or a patient at the end of her rope? At that point I didn't care why he had stopped; I was ready to seize the moment.

I told him I was wondering about the long wait, and I expressed my frustration. He looked like a businessman in a hurry, so I told him as succinctly as possible why I was there. He listened, left, and then came back to sit down with me. He told me he had checked on my situation, and that I would be helped shortly.

Then, in a friendly way he asked, "So, what's your experience been in my hospital?"

His hospital? (Was this God come down from heaven?) It turned out his name was Michael Guiry, and he was a vice president at Holy Name Hospital. He sat quietly, his hands clasped in front of him, and listened.

"I don't understand the way cancer patients are treated," I said. "It's not just me, it's all of us! Not only are we fighting cancer, we are fighting excessive wait times, appointment times that aren't honored, and calls that never get returned. And once we get to see a doctor, they act like we're an imposition; we've interrupted their day. And if you dare to ask a question? Well, forget it! We're the ones fighting for our lives, and the healthcare profession treats us like we are the ones who are imposing on them!"

Maybe I unloaded too much, but Michael Guiry continued to listen intently. As he got up to leave, he gave me his contact information and said, "I'm running to a meeting now, and I sure hope when I get out of it you won't still be in this waiting room. Please let me know how your appointment went, because I really want to know. Your experiences will help to make us a better hospital. All I can say is, I'm so sorry for what you've been through. I know it's probably not much comfort now, but I hope I've been able to help to make things a little better for you today."

We never met in person again, but behind the scenes I know he was helping me. Sadly, for Holy Name Medical Center Hospital (and its patients), he has moved on. But from what I understand, he is still deeply involved in hospital administration and in building great healthcare facilities that truly serve their patients.

****

As it turned out, Michael Guiry was a brief stop, a refreshing cup of water, on a cancer battle that had many, many miles to go, and continues to this day.

From the beginning, I have been up for the challenge, ready to do my part. What doesn't seem to register with the health profession is that patients are not only dealing with cancer, and other deadly diseases, but also the daily pressures of ordinary life. Family and friends need attention. There are crushing monthly bills, groceries to buy, and plumbing to fix. All the minutiae of daily life continues—and with it there is the resistant, broken body to pull through the day. As for me, I have a left arm that's always in pain from my shoulder to the tip of my fingers. I have a sore butt, sore bones, hot flashes, and fatigue—all the lovely side effects of the latest new drug. I do not complain. I refuse to let cancer interfere with living my life to its fullest. But still ....

Here is an example of a day in the life of living with cancer:

The day before I was scheduled for an important PET scan, power went out in my neighborhood. I spent a cold, sleepless night, tossing and turning. Morning came, and I pulled myself together for the long-awaited test. One good thing—I was glad the prep wasn't complicated: the only information I was given about how to prepare for the test was: "Eat protein!" Okay, that I can do.

I arrived at the PET scan location, groggy from lack of sleep and thrown off by the lack of lights and heat in the house. Dutifully, I got ready to follow the white-coated receptionist into the first holding room. I knew there would be a number of these holding rooms before the test began.

But this time, the woman peered into the computer, looking confused. "There is a problem here," she said. "The pre-authorization form I have doesn't line up with the codes in my computer. I can't register you until I am able to get others to figure this out."

"You cannot make me wait today while you sort this mess out," I said, my temper rising. "I cannot go through this again!"

She disappeared, and I called Michael Guiry on my cellphone and left a message that, once again, everything appeared to be all screwed up.

Ten minutes later, the registration lady was back and apologetic. Unfortunately, the computer codes were still an issue, but since I was cleared for the PET scan anyway, I could have the test while the computer problem was being sorted out.

I am convinced Michael Guiry received my voicemail message

and told them not to detain me. For the hundredth time, I thank my lucky stars that I met him.

I was escorted down yet another long, nondescript hall to the PET scan department, where they arranged me like a slab of meat on a table. But my spirits rose when the radiation technologist, a lovely young woman with pink nails and a bouncy personality, smiled, looked me in the eye, and asked in a direct and friendly way, "What are the last things you had to eat and drink before today?"

By that time, I was like a weary and delayed passenger who just felt her plane lift off the ground after spending hours on the tarmac. Nothing could stop me now! My spirits were rising, and I was ready for anything.

"Oh, nothing but coffee with a little milk at 7:00 a.m.," I replied.

Her face fell. "You had coffee with milk this morning? Excuse me, I will be right back."

Ten minutes later she reappeared, bearing bad news. Nobody told me—until she did that moment—that a little milk interferes with the PET scan.

The test would have to be delayed for at least half a day.

I have endured far more before. But on this day, at this time, after everything else, the sleepless night before, the anticipation and hope of good news, and the bracing for the bad—I did something I hadn't done in all my years of fighting cancer.

I wept.

****

Dr. Giuseppe C.? How can I write the story of my cancer without a mention of the human obstacle I will call Dr. Giuseppe C.?

He came with a good recommendation from my excellent plastic surgeon, Dr. D'Amico, and that made me inclined to trust him.

But flags went up almost immediately. The minute he walked into the room, he exuded pride and over-confidence. He was clearly intent on winning me over. (Had he been told I was "demanding?" That I expected to be treated like an equal?) In any case, I felt I was in the presence of a slick salesman.

It's awkward enough to disrobe (physically and figuratively) in front of a stranger, but Dr. Giuseppe C. made it worse by praising my "beautiful, moisturized skin" and comparing me with his other patients, whose skin was all dried out and flaky. When he finally got around to giving his treatment recommendation, it consisted of a series of infusions jabbed in my buttocks.

Later, I was leaving one of my early infusion treatments and getting into my car in the parking lot when my phone rang. It was Dr. Giuseppe C. He was furious, berating me for not following up with the protocols associated with the infusions. He was also furious I had not gotten back to him in the prescribed period of time.

"What are you talking about?" I said, amazed. "I'm doing the infusions as you recommended. You never told me about any follow-up protocols …"

"You are lying!" the doctor shouted. The slick salesman was no more. "I gave you specific instructions, and you have disregarded them; you never responded to our messages. If you cared about your health, you would have followed my instructions!"

There it was again. "If I cared about my health …" The accusation was irrational, unsupportable.

I was alive precisely because I care about my health.

****

And then it was November 2016. For a month, I had been feeling another lump above my clavicle, which I was pretty sure was a cancerous lymph node. I got an appointment with another oncologist affiliated with Hackensack Hospital, Dr. Deena Graham. Her resume was impressive, and I sent her my medical files.

At the appointment, she walked into the examining room like a small tornado and delivered startling news.

"Since we both know you have stage IV metastasized cancer, the question is how we treat you," she said. "Of course, it's a matter of managing your disease, because at this point there is no cure."

I was speechless. What's this about metastasized cancer? I had localized recurring cancer.

Didn't I?

I asked her how she knew I had stage IV cancer even before examining me or getting a biopsy of the lump above my clavicle.

"Well, Deborah, it's right here in your pathology report of February 2015. It says the cancer has penetrated your skin, and that is stage IV cancer."

February 2015! I told her that since that February I had seen two oncologists, and neither of them told me I had stage IV cancer. Everything they said and led me to believe, was that I had recurrent regional or recurrent local cancer. What's more, each of them had continued to treat me with drugs that obviously hadn't worked.

That was eighteen months ago. I didn't want to think of the time lost.

"What are the survival statistics for someone like me?"

"Two to three years is the average," she replied, her voice careful and even.

It was like watching my life flash before my eyes. How much time spent—how much time lost! Running through the rain to find the wonderful Dr. Richard D'Amico. The successful breast reconstruction. The stress of sitting for hours on end in sticky chairs, waiting for the words, "Dr. X will see you now." The doctors who were too overworked to be anything but nasty. The misunderstandings ("You had coffee and milk this morning? Sorry, we can't do the test, you have to come back ...")

Even as I asked it, I knew my next question was naive and unnecessary, but I asked it anyway.

"So, Doctor, is that survival rate two to three years from right now—or two to three years from February 2015?"

Here was the final irony: For nearly ten years, I had worked hard to be my own best advocate. I had studied medical research papers and challenged men and women with advanced medical degrees. I had done everything I could to improve my own healthcare. Now I was asking a question whose answer was so clear, so obvious, and so final.

"Deborah," she replied, "I think you are smarter than that."

Chapter Eleven

The "Gardeners"

As a child I cherished Madeline, the classic book series about the French girl who set her boarding school upside down. Madeline was brave and intrepid, always bursting through the walls of the ordinary. To be just one of "twelve little girls in twelve straight lines"? Not Madeline. "Nothing frightens Madeline," starts one review, "not tigers, not mice, not even getting sick. To Madeline, a trip to the hospital is a grand adventure."

Even as a child I knew: Madeline was me. I was the rebel in the Ethiopian cave, and the girl who galloped with Sa'id through a land of hyenas and lions. Like Madeline, I was the loner, fighting the straitjacket of boarding school. No matter what blows have come my way—the alienation of my parents, the betrayal of love, even deadly cancer—I have taken on each challenge as a grand adventure that required only the most straightforward response: "Okay, let's get on with it."

Few people have been ready to make that journey with me. Right from the beginning, as a child and a young woman, I rarely fit in. I never had an interest in the girlie things like makeup, clothes, shopping, or gossip. I'm sure growing up as the ambassador's daughter gave me a unique take on reality, but so did my own objective way of thinking. For as long as I can remember, what really absorbs me are politics, world economics, and being interested in everything—from what makes individuals tick to the state of the world.

Of course, there were other complexities in my psyche. I'm sure that because of my parent's rejection, I began life as insecure girl who was eager to be liked, accepted, and needed. But I learned very quickly to build my confidence by looking outside myself, being interested in ideas, and helping others. That's why I am impatient and rather contemptuous of people who are self-absorbed and selfish. I'm sure I recognize echoes of my mother in those qualities. Unlike Mummy, I have always tried to think and care about others, even to the point of rescuing someone when they needed it.

Likewise, the kind of friends who have attracted me throughout my life are independent, confident, unselfish, curious about the world, and … interesting.

I cannot end my book without paying tribute to these friends. They came into my life as their own people, living their own lives, yet along the way, they nourished mine. I have been completely happy as a loner and a lover of solitude, but I let these friends scale the walls of my fortress, and they have made me even happier. People like these deserve kudos and gratitude.

The French writer Proust described these kinds of people as "les jardiniers qui pour faire notre ames fleurir" (the gardeners who make our souls bloom).

****

My lasting friendships can be divided into the friends I made at work and outside of work. Tucked in between, like pressed flowers in a book, are those fleeting friendships that nevertheless made a lasting impact in my life and memory: Elena in Ethiopia, my fellow student who died in a plane crash two years after I met her; Joyce, who was a runner-up to the title of Miss Chile, but who died from breast cancer approximately twelve years ago; Viviana, Sonja, Leslie, and Marisol (also from Chile), with whom I've had little contact since the 1970s, but still remember fondly.

In recent years, I've had the great pleasure of reconnecting with friends from this era. Now, as I count up the many varieties in my garden, I am filled with gratitude for this long litany of women and men who have brought joy into my life, from so many places around the world:

I have two wonderful Bulgarian friends, Elena & Zornitza. Fom Ireland: Siobhan, my cara (the beautiful Gaelic word for friend), and Adrian, Siobhan, Sabdh, and Niamh—my special Irish family.

Tia is my wonderful friend from England, and from America, I especially want to mention Maureen, Margaret, Alene, Gail, Mary-Ann, and Lauren.

There is Florian, a talented Frenchman whose name will also be familiar to many TV viewers (as I will explain further in the next chapter); Fernando, a handsome, Michael Bolton look-alike from Chile, and my Dominican-American friend, Gianna, my amiga del alma (friend of the heart) as we refer to each other. Then there is Francesca, who courageously left her home in Romania, and Angelika, my friend from Armenia who became an American entrepreneur and founded a company, Loveloveedibles, that makes delicious, unbaked power foods and cakes.

And how can I forget Jimmy, Tom, and Kari Anne's husband, Yiannis?

As I hear their names, I remember again how each of these men and women are dear to me, each in their own way.

****

Then there are those people who fit in no category at all. For me, there is just one: Emily Stanbury, a.k.a. Nursie our English nanny, who made life stringent and hard—but in many ways also opened up worlds to me.

Yes, in her own way, Nursie was a gardener who made my soul bloom.

I have included photographs of Nursie in this book. The photos show a smiling blonde woman with a strong English chin and sturdy, athletic frame. In her early years, she was quite pretty, and from the pictures she looks relaxed and fun-loving. Who would guess I butted heads with Nursie all the time?

Yes, life with Nursie was pretty much one long boot camp, but I loved her. She was the epitome of the brisk, no-nonsense English nanny. She could be playful and stern; she was also tough and creative. Although I couldn't help but feel she loved all of us, she loved Alexandra unreservedly.

As for me, I'm pretty sure Nursie thought of me as an untamable nuisance. I was the charge that was difficult and burdensome. Charge (the term British nannies use to refer to the children they care for) is a good description of the grating, sand-papery relationship between us. And yet, through Nursie, my creativity was let loose. She taught me how to make all sorts of things, from lavender sachets to knitting a sweater. Thanks to Nursie I have excellent posture, good manners, a spot-on memory, and a disciplined journal-writing habit (the Brits are especially fond of diary-keeping). So, I have many things to be grateful to her for.

But I wonder if Nursie didn't have secrets and heartaches, because she lived so carefully, always staying between the lines of what was proper and correct. Behind her British reserve, I sensed that Nursie felt and cared deeply, and I was curious to know more about her. Even as a child, I wanted to know what made people tick, and the reasons they ended up being who they were.

So, of course, I was curious about Nursie, and one day I asked her about her life when she was young. (As I've mentioned earlier, she had been nanny to the Sulzbergers, the legendary owners and publishers of The New York Times since the 1880s).

Nursie answered my question carefully:

She had loved someone once. I understood her to say she had lost someone in the War. She didn't say anything more than that, but it was enough. I was a child who knew what it was to be alone, to love solitude, to feel the bitterness of rejection, and her small, careful confidence brought Nursie into sharper focus for me. From her guarded answer, I pieced together the rest: She had been a young woman during World War II (perhaps that was when her lover had died), and after that she closed off that part of her heart forever. Though I'm sure she loved all of us in her own way, my sister Alexandra was the child she never had.

When Alexandra was getting ready to go off to college, Nursie went back to England, where she worked for Cy Sulzberger's daughter, whom she had raised. Now she was raising a second generation of Sulzberger children. After a few years, Nursie moved back to her hometown in Devon, England. However, she and Alexandra remained in very close touch, by phone and letters, and we all stayed part of Nursie's life to the extent that she regularly wrote newsy, caring letters to us about her life in England. In return, we sent letters to her about our own lives. After all, we were her family.

Nursie died in June 2010 at age ninety-three. Several years before she had suffered a stroke that left her bedridden and unable to speak. To think of that strong, vigorous personality—left powerless and alone! When I heard the news, I cried. No more lovely letters, no more possibility of hearing her clipped English accent in the next room or on the telephone. My thoughts went immediately to Alexandra, because I knew my sister's heart had broken. Nursie had been a real mother to her. After the stroke, Alexandra was not only a frequent visitor, but she made sure all of Nursie's needs were met and watched over her with the tenderness of a loving daughter.

Alexandra was the only one of our family to attend Nursie's funeral.

****

Unforgettable and lasting work friendships

Fuad—My boss at UNICEF in New York. It was a very sad day saying goodbye to Fuad. He was taking a post in Vietnam, and I would gladly have continued to work for him, but UNICEF barred me—as a young American woman—from being assigned a post in Africa. That policy led me to resign from one of the best jobs I had ever had and forced me to leave one of my best bosses ever.

Fuad had become like a surrogate father and brother to me (although he probably would have hated to be thought of as fatherly, given his commitment to health and youth). He was twenty years older than I, but he had a youthful appearance and many interests to match. They had a scope that was truly remarkable, ranging from the physically strenuous activities to the most thoughtful of pursuits: he was a very good tennis player, and he was just as passionate about his stamp collecting hobby.

On our last day, we hugged, and I fought back tears, because I knew that I would probably never see him again.

"Thank you for believing in me," I said, trying to keep my voice even and professional. "No one ever believed in me before. And besides, you have been a wonderful mentor and a friend!"

"I have total confidence in you," Fuad said. I could tell he was trying to keep his voice jaunty and cheerful, even though saying goodbye was hard for him too. He told me that what he wanted most for me was to be happy and personally fulfilled.

I will never forget the beautiful recommendation letter he wrote for me. At the risk of blowing my own horn too vigorously, I would like to quote from it, because I think it shows Fuad's great care over my future, and the trust we had established between us:

"It is a tribute to Deborah's dynamism, eagerness to learn, personal attributes, and professional interest that she quickly assimilates," Fuad wrote. "She demonstrated initiative, ability to work under pressure, willingness to put in excess time, capability of finding solutions to problems, and established and maintained excellent working relations with colleagues at all levels from all countries. Her proficiency in English, Spanish, and French facilitated her work in the international environment. The quality and quantity of her work were irreproachable. She demonstrated exceptional loyalty and devotion, a willingness to assist colleagues at all times, and a genuine interest and concern for the ideals of UNICEF, an empathy with the problems of development in the Third World, and human qualities of the highest level."

Well, I was wrong about one thing. We did see each other again, even though it was twenty-seven years later. Fuad was living in Canada, and our paths finally intersected again at a UNICEF event. He looked the same, except that his hair had turned white. He was happy, still involved with organizing UNICEF alumni reunions, writing articles on UNICEF, stamp collecting, traveling, and—of course—playing tennis.

Bob Byrne—My boss at Kwasha Lipton: an actuarial and benefits consulting firm. At KL, Bob showed me the best of the profit-making world. He was wholesome, unassuming, and true-blue as the summer sky. He had married his high school sweetheart, had five kids, and then adopted two more. He coached his kids' softball and basketball teams and centered his life around his family. He never cared about power and position—he cared about his employees, just like he cared about his family. Nobody could make Bob fit in a box—not even in his appearance. I can still see him in his business suit and trademark yellow Converse sneakers!

Bob made our work environment happy; his philosophy was it was possible to have fun while you were doing serious work. With Bob in charge, we had summer picnics, barbecues, and holiday parties. He arranged KL backgammon and chess clubs, and provided employees with every amenity, including laundry services and massage therapy sessions.

KL's golden age ended when it was sold to Coopers & Lybrand, then to PriceWaterhouse, and finally to Mellon Bank. That's when I left, and Bob left too. With that, the special work culture created by Bob Byrne simply vanished. However, there are still echoes of that great place in our regular KL reunions, and in my twice-a-year catch-up lunches with Bob. I am grateful we are still in touch, and that we always will be.

Patsy—A Brazilian-American girl with a stunning pedigree and a California-Dreamin' quality about her. I met Patsy at UNICEF. Her maternal grandfather was Ellsworth Bunker, best known as US Ambassador to South Vietnam from 1967-73. Her father was a famous Brazilian heart surgeon. Patsy was a tall, natural, stunning beauty, a fabulous tennis player, and she swam gracefully with the 1970s in crowd that included James Caan, Jack Nicholson, and other

Hollywood stars. Eventually, she took up with a married Russian diplomat. To stay off the radar of the CIA and KGB, she used my apartment as their rendezvous point. Yet, Patsy was down-to-earth and natural, and some of my fondest memories are spending ski weekends at her grandfather's dairy farm in Vermont.

Judi—She was the English friend I met while working at UNICEF. We instantly connected through our love of the world and our commitment to helping the less fortunate. Judi was one of the first westerners to live in China. She transferred there when UNICEF opened a new office and lived there with a small ex-pat community in primitive surroundings. We lost touch for thirty years and reconnected only six years ago. It was as if the years between had vanished—and our last conversation had been just the day before. Judi is a beautiful woman inside and out. I'm glad she sought me out after all these years.

Geri—We became friends while working together at Kwasha Lipton. We got pregnant at the same time too. I lost my child; Geri didn't. I became Auntie Deborah to Geri's two girls. For years, I took the girls shopping for their birthdays and Christmas. On those days they were "my girls". Today we rarely see each other, but the bond of friendship will always be there.

Lidya - We met while working together at Coopers & Lybrand about 1999 and really connected over our mutual love of a popular Spanish-language soap opera. Lidya, who emigrated from the Dominican Republic, is one of the sweetest, kindest people I know. She's blessed with an amazing voice. Anytime I get to hear her sing, it brings joy to my soul.

Maria from Pennsylvania - A beautiful, well-educated career girl from Argentina with two teenage girls and always two dogs (at least). No matter how busy her life is she always takes time for others. She connects with me on both a professional and personal level, and she's always interested in what I am doing and how I am. To know Maria is to love her!

Norma - She came to the US from Argentina with her husband fifty years ago, but I didn't meet her until the 1990s. Even though we communicate mostly by email, our friendship is fully three-dimensional. We share a passionate interest in how the world is behaving, and Norma's mind is so alert and insightful, I think she could make a name for herself in the media, doing political commentary. She is not only intelligent, but a beautiful and inspiring woman. I respect, adore, and cherish her as the best of pen pals.

Audrey—My oldest friend. We met at UNICEF in the late 1970s. I will always be Debbie to her, because that is how she heard my name when we were introduced, and she has called me that ever since. We connected immediately as citizens of the world. Audrey is a Venezuelan-American, and like me, she is well educated and speaks three languages. We shared UNICEF, three languages (English, Spanish, and French), the Sunday New York Times crossword puzzle, and interests that ranged from books to newspapers to foreign films. Audrey was one of my bridesmaids at my first wedding in 1982, and my maid of honor at wedding #2 in 1995.

In our thirty-seven-year friendship I have seen Audrey through many challenges: The tragic death of her two young brothers; her father's stroke; the death of her mother, Itala (with whom I was close), and the ten years of medical suffering her husband endured, which ended with his death. I have been Audrey's shoulder to lean on and her travel companion. Together we made a historic visit to Cuba in 2014, where we visited Hemingway's home, Finca Vigia. We dined at his favorite restaurant and explored Havana's faded but historic streets in a '57 Chevy. I love her, and I will always be her little sister Debbie.

Karen G—We met in 1989, at the healthcare company we worked for in Englewood Cliffs, New Jersey, and became instant friends. We also are companions in cancer: Karen's began in 2007 and mine in 2008, and our journey has only drawn us closer. But my image of Karen will always be the first sight of her thirty years ago, a beautiful, impeccably dressed woman wearing red lipstick. Karen is the original meaning of the Jewish Mom—generous, caring, and kind. The happiness of others is what she wants most. How glad I was to do something for her—I introduced her to her husband without ever knowing it.

We were sharing a weekend in the Hamptons, where we ended up sitting in the hotel's lounge next to a man dressed in tennis whites. I invited him to join us for a night on the town, and later, sensing a sizzle, I left them alone, hoping for fireworks to happen. (Boom!) The following year they were married, and soon after their precious daughter, Emma, was born. Today, Karen and I are not just cancer survivors, but soldiers in the fight. Only those fighting a daily battle with the disease, like Karen and me, have a true understanding of it. Unlike most people, we are proactive about our treatments, and we research everything. There is nothing we won't do for each other. There is no other way to say it: I love Karen deeply. Friends forever.

Friends I made away from work, forever and lasting

Kari Anne—My beautiful, caring Norwegian Pan Am flight attendant friend! True Viking and Closet California Girl, all rolled into one. I met Kari Anne through one of my old roommates, Lee. We bonded instantly on the laughter-filled night when Kari Anne demonstrated her cross-country skiing techniques by gliding, in high heels, across our living room floor. I connect with non-American women very easily, but the connection with Kari Anne is a cut above. She was—and is—a true Viking: tough, ferocious, strong willed, secure, opinionated, and loyal to a 'T', with a deep attachment to her Norse homeland, her family, and her culture. I've always admired her self-assuredness, her ability to never bend to the whims of others, and her strong sense of self. No weakness allowed. We laugh, we have fun, and we share good times and bad. Easter celebrations at Kari Anne's home in Connecticut were one of my favorite invitations of the year, and even though I was her only non-Pan Am, non-Scandinavian friend: I fit in, I was welcomed, and I was loved. To give back is easy: I love Kari Anne deeply.

Nancy—She is the sister-in-law of Rob, the man I dated for nearly a decade; that relationship didn't last, but Nancy's friendship has. When I think of Nancy I think of the words stylish, easy going, and beautiful. She is a woman with a wonderful sense of humor, the best laugh, and an Italian heritage that is open and welcoming. Nancy is a hairdresser who owned her own salon, so—of course— her hair always looks great. She is an expert cook and generous with her hospitality. Her Christmas Eve parties are always exquisite and memorable, and they have made me actually fond of Christmas. We became very close friends around 2005, and I see her more than anyone else. We share a love of consignment shops, overnight trips, plays, concerts, and making last-minute plans. We try out new res-taurants and enjoy listening to her brother, a jazz-singer, perform. We meet for weekly dinners with our spouses. Even sweeter, our husbands bonded in 2013, and so we've had happy times traveling together as couples. Nancy is all about family, and so I was touched when she asked if she could accompany me to Sudbury, MA to at-tend my Aunt Betty's ninetieth birthday party. I visit with her elder-ly mother, Filomena, and have had the quiet joy of singing old Ital-ian songs with her, which gives me peace and pleasure and warms my soul. When I think of Nancy, this lovely Italian phrase comes to mind—La amo amica mia!

Jackie from Tuxedo Park, NY— I met Jackie through my husband, Dixon. We didn't become friends until 2013 or '14. She is fiercely independent and set in her ways. Jackie is the epitome of the inde-pendent, no-nonsense woman—completely disinterested in what others think of her and unafraid to speak her mind. I love the fact that she's completely comfortable with who she is. Jackie is fiercely loyal and easy to be around, and while it's not always easy to travel with friends, traveling with Jackie was easy. She found out I was going on a last-minute trip to Costa Rica and quickly said, "I'd like to go with you". That last-minute trip, in 2017, turned out to be perfect. I couldn't have asked for a better, or easier-going, travel companion.

The writer Mark Twain is supposed to have said that the best way to find out if you like someone or hate them is to travel with them. Well, I traveled with Jackie, and I found out that yes—I not only like her—I love her.

The sister I never had

Karen C—She and her husband Tom lived opposite my parents' townhouse in The Gates at Quail Hollow in Charlotte, North Carolina. Even before I knew her, when my father was dying, it was Karen who jumped in to help so my mother could be with Papa at the hospice. When our family gathered for my father's memorial service in March 2003 (we didn't have a funeral because my father was nonreligious—an agnostic), we all arranged to stay at different places. My husband and I stayed with Karen and Tom. That's how our friendship began.

Karen is a tall, beautiful, elegant woman with three grown children and eight grandchildren. At first, I couldn't believe she was taking the time to be with me. She is the sister I always wanted and never had. No—more than that—Karen is a friend, sister, mother, grandmother, mentor, and adviser—and also the most caring and giving woman I've ever known. The solitary child in the cave, the little girl shut out from her parents' lives—that little girl can run to Karen, and Karen understands. I trust her in a way I have never trusted anyone, before or since. Karen makes me feel safe and loved. My instinct is usually to fall into the role of caretaker, but Karen is the friend who takes care of me. She checks on me all the time, and she never shrinks from giving me her honest opinion. She questions me, praises me, advises me, criticizes me, and dissects me— and I welcome it all. Like a true sister, there are no boundaries, and no fear of being exposed, abandoned, or lied about. We share our deepest secrets, our pasts, our pains, our frustrations, our successes, our failures, and our disappointments.

In Karen, I found a "me." And in finding me, Karen found more of herself. Whatever my future holds, I know she will be there. It isn't possible to love a human being more than I love Karen.

****

These are the gardeners who make my soul bloom. As I see them all assembled here, I think: What a range of personalities and interests! How well they reflect the many, and different, facets of my personality and my life! One by one, I examine the role of each of these cherished friends in my life.

I am satisfied.

Chapter Twelve

Odds and Ends

How do you compress your life between covers of a book? As I review what I have written so far, I realize there is so much more I have to say. In one way, life is chronological, but in another way (which is equally real), life is made up of events and memories that are woven throughout the years. They form patterns that are as vivid today as when they happened, and they can be examined at any time.

Likewise, I cherish certain individuals, even though they are not always present in my everyday life. Between the covers of a book they may fit in no particular place, but they fit everywhere, too. Their journeys and their lives are important to me. People, ideas, impressions, and memories—these are all worth examining, even if for just a moment. Whether you are examining a beautiful woven fabric, or opening a box of treasures, some pieces you linger over, and others you give a fleeting glance and fold away or put back in the box. Either way, every single thing and person is important.

In other words, these are my life's precious odds and ends.

****

My philosophy of life: Live to the fullest! Staying positive is my mantra. Spending a minute, an hour, or a day worrying about things that may happen, or worrying and focusing on those things that have gone awry, are of no interest to me. They are solely a waste of time and energy. In the most difficult of times, I am able to use my inner strength to overcome any negative thoughts. I always think of those less fortunate; of those who lack the most basic of life's needs; of those with missing limbs; without sight; with no food, shelter, or family; and those who never make it past eight years of age. Feeling sorry for myself or worrying about things is foreign to me.

Someone once wrote, "You don't become happy by pursuing happiness, but rather by living a life that is meaningful. Happiness is a byproduct, not a primary goal. Happiness is a butterfly. Stop chasing it. Busy yourself with meaningful, productive things, and it will sneak up on you and perch on your shoulder."

****

The challenge of cancer: At this moment, writing this in late 2017, I am tuckered out and more than mildly annoyed. I have just learned that none of my recent cancer therapies have worked. My physician, Dr. Deena Graham (a rare physician with talent and common sense) has assigned a combo of two chemo drugs to start now, in December 2017. No other treatments have worked. Lucky me. We'll see if I have any veins left after this. In more than one way, this is my last shot.

So much time wasted before I met Dr. Deena! I have none to spare, and I remember each useless round of therapy with cynicism and resentment. I know now, from personal experience, that the state of medicine in this country is appalling. Virtually all healthcare decisions are made to contain costs and avoid litigation. Government regulations block the use of truly promising drugs and therapies. The whole healthcare system has been reconfigured. Few physicians are willing to think out of the box anymore to help a patient. First, because they often are blocked from helping by the rules, and second, if they are allowed to move forward—and they are wrong—they risk their reputations and livelihoods. However, I do not feel particularly sorry for them. For me, and for every other cancer patient, our greatest risk is in a category all its own: life itself.

But these are only frustrations. My mindset remains as constant as it was when I got my first cancer diagnosis nine years ago: Okay. It is what it is. Let's get on with it. I simply do not waste time with woe-is-me thinking. I'm sure my outlook was knitted into place in my childhood, when I faced the incomprehensible: my parents didn't care about me. At an early age, I was forced to understand I would have to figure out life all by myself, and for the most part, figuring out life has produced wonderful fruit. It has brought me cherished friendships, many adventures, great fun, and—all in all—much fulfillment, both personal and professional. Besides, lone wolves have steely spines. I can take on whatever comes—even cancer. So yes, let's get on with it.

****

The joy of physical challenge: I have found that happiness and fulfilled life is the simple, direct pleasure of having command over my body. Most directly, that means exercise and enjoying the great outdoors. These pursuits have always played a big part in my life. I have been repaid with all the classic benefits of exercise and healthy outdoor living—namely appearance, better health, and a stronger body. But I never expected these things would also help after breast cancer surgery. According to my plastic surgeon, my strong muscular chest wall gave him the structure to start rebuilding my breasts twice as quickly.

My love of exercise and the outdoors began in childhood. In Ethiopia, these pursuits were completely fulfilled. I plunged into every sport available—soccer, roller blading, tennis, horseback riding, and track and field. I won many first, second, and third place medals in track and field. By the time I was eleven or twelve years old, I had reached my full height and was faster and taller than many of the Ethiopian girls. In Chile, I added another sport to my regimen—field hockey. But I wasn't done yet. As I got older, I learned to ski, and I loved the freedom and challenge of taking long hikes, wherever I was. As long as it was outdoors, that was good enough for me.

My love of the outdoors also extends to the quieter, more contemplative side of it, like gardening. There is something about plunging my hands in dirt—I love the cool moistness and the strong, iron-y fragrance of dirt. I find it energizing to mold this elemental part of the earth in my hands—and plant seeds that will grow into something beautiful.

So, I love the outdoors—yet, I am also completely happy indoors, especially in an exercise studio environment. Many people dread hauling themselves off to exercise—well, I thrive in an exercise environment. I consider exercise to be a mental as well as physical. No matter how busy I am, I always make time to exercise.

My employer in the 1990s, the consulting firm Kwasha Lipton, had a gym. It opened up a new world of disciplined exercise for me. Am I an overachiever? Probably! I enlisted Bill, the gym manager, to be my personal trainer. Before the crack of dawn, I was driving to his house to make a one-hour private class at five a.m. Later, when I was working in New York City, I hired a personal trainer, Nick, to come to my house four days a week for a private session. "Pretty expensive," friends would say.

"Yes, Nick is my car payment," I would reply. It was true—I held on to my old car for seventeen years in order to continue my work-outs with Nick.

Then, inevitably, the time came when we both had to move on. That's when I discovered The Bar Method. It combines dance with core conditioning, yoga, Pilates, and weight training. It is based on a system created by a German-born dance instructor, Lotte Berk, who founded The Bar Method in 1959. The Bar Method has be-come one of my major passions. It has toned my body, given me flexibility and strength, and reversed my osteoporosis. The payback came almost as soon as I began, because I not only lost inches but became the most flexible I've ever been. Imagine, doing splits in my late 50s and early 60s!

As if there needed to be another bonus, there is one: the teach-ers. My Bar Method teachers are the loveliest, most talented, inspi-rational, and caring group of women I have ever known. Bar clients are very special too. A few have even become good friends: Gianna, Francesca, and Angelika. The list goes on.

My current cancer condition has forced me to put Bar on the side burner for a while, but I refuse to concede the fight. I'm hoping to get back to Bar soon, because I know exercise is what keeps our bones strong and our minds clear.

****

My love of animals: From my childhood on, I always had animals in my life. In the early years, in Ethiopia, Chile, and beyond, I cher-ished my dogs (the restless Ajax, for a while, but especially Prince, who was as regal and noble as his name). And I will never forget our stable of horses in Addis Ababa, and the impatient thrill I al-ways felt when I ran into that musty barn and caught a grin and a greeting from Sa'id. "Good morning, Debritu!" he would say—and I prepared to saddle up Whiskey, my beautiful gray. No, he was not technically my horse, but I thought of him that way, because Whiskey took me on great adventures. Together we set off into the rough and raw backcountry of Addis Ababa, with Sa'id as my companion and guardian.

Today, I live far away from the sub-Sahara (though I visit often in my thoughts) and my choice of favorite animals has changed as well. For the past twenty-one years, I have given my affection not to dogs or horses, but to cats. Specifically, one cat—Oreo—so named because she is black and white—a sweet confection of chocolate and frosting. Although just a housecat (those fussy and pretentious exotic breeds aren't for me), Oreo has reached the advanced age of twenty-one, and I think of her as my geriatric cat. Maybe my affinity for animals has been like a magic elixir, extending Oreo's life? No, I will give her all the credit. But with long life comes all the infirmities of old age. Oreo constantly whines, she has high blood pressure and a thyroid condition, and my formerly polite and lady-like cat now does her business wherever she feels like it, including the living room rug. Perhaps a long life isn't always best.

But if life ebbs and flows, it is always renewing itself too. And so, it has with my newest edition of cat, Sparkles. She is a six-year-old cat with a sweet disposition and the black and white coloring of a tuxedo. Sparkles belonged to my mother-in-law, Sara, until Sara had a stroke in 2017 and could no longer live on her own. Sara moved to an apartment with a full-time caregiver and cats weren't allowed, so Dixon took her on. Polite as she is, Sparkles has tried to befriend Oreo, but it's been Oreo's territory for so long that Oreo (cranky in her old age) won't have anything to do with her. But Sparkles sails on, serene and happy every day. She is lovable and so easy. Still, I think in her contented demeanor runs a streak of courage. Sparkles is not afraid.

****

The company of men: My memories are filled with many wonderful men, smart men, and good-looking men. I went out with a lot of them. It's not that I slept around—I didn't. I simply enjoy men's company. I'm sure the men (and women) we allow into our lives are in many ways a reflection of our upbringing and our relationship with our parents, and it certainly was that way with me. Yes, my father and I had a difficult and complicated relationship, but I never stopped loving and admiring him. He was a man of great talent, intellect, and sheer zest for life, and in many ways, he set the standard for me when it came to the men I allowed in my life.

I have always been attracted to men who are intellectually stimulating, and interested and involved in the world, just as I am. At the same time, I always circled around the finality of commitment, and I'm sure that stemmed from the alienation I felt from my father, because he made it clear I was not important to him. So, I became the lone wolf, always roaming the perimeter of life, never really looking to settle down. And to be honest about it, I couldn't believe any man could actually be interested in me. Why would any man love me? My father didn't. I ran. My heart was always whispering to my head, "Don't give him a chance to hurt you."

So, most of my relationships were vivid, but brief. The minute a man showed a real interest in me, I ran. This turned out to be a boon for my friends. "Well, if you aren't interested in him, Deborah, I am!" That's how I unwittingly became a matchmaker for many of my friends. But while it lasted, each relationship, each romance, left a lovely, lingering memory for me.

There was Jim, Larry, Jeff, Guccio ... and Cristian.

Cristian. Perhaps there's a little sadness attached to this memory. Cristian was a Chilean diplomat. When we met in New York, he was separated from his wife, who happened to be the daughter of my mother's secretary in Chile. I was later blamed for ruining their marriage. All not true! I was in my early 20s, and our friendship only developed after he'd left Wife #1. But no one who discovered our innocent relationship (like my father and mother) were interested in the facts. It was just one more thing my parents added to their list of terrible things I had done: I had stolen a man from his wife! Even more painful (as I only learned years later), they shared my supposed and nonexistent indiscretions with anyone who would listen.

At the time, I didn't care what they thought. Cristian fascinated me. He was worldly and intelligent, with a wonderful sense of humor. He had lived all over the world and spoke several languages. Our conversations were lively and stimulating, never boring. We spent hours together talking about the world, about books, enjoying a good meal and fine wine. Plus, I know he loved me.

And now my thoughts are drawn back to another special man, Pablo. I met him one Halloween night while out with a friend. Pablo was a smart, down-to-earth, giving, affectionate, all-around man. He was interested in living life to its fullest. We shared a similar love of nature, wine, music, food, and the world around us. And yes, he was another man who really loved me, who showed me that I was worthy of love.

As for my first husband, Johnny? The years have not erased his charming bad boy image. He still has a restless streak—moving to California, then zigzagging to Florida to run a boating brokerage firm. Since our marriage ended in the 1980s, he has had many girlfriends, and many of them have posted not-so-nice things on social media that suggest their time with him was no better than mine. He remains the ultimate salesperson, with lots of charm and effervescence, though for many of us his charm eventually goes flat. Funny enough, he is dogged by the same old demon that he had when we met—deep personal insecurity, which is only held at bay when he gets a lot of attention.

I still run into Rob, the man I lived with for a decade, because of my close relationship with his brother, Jimmy, and his wife, Nancy—who is my dear friend. Rob has gone through a few relationships since we were together. His last two relationships were with women from Costa Rica. At age seventy-one, Rob maintains his zest for life.

Rob used hard work and ambition to fortify his blue-collar roots, and eventually he became a member of the legendary 1% club. After his son graduated from college, Rob turned over his business to him, so he could pursue his love of travel. Among his favorite places to visit are his own properties—he has an estate in Goshen, CT; a place in Key Largo, Florida; and a time share in Saint Thomas, Virgin Islands. If he isn't building or redoing one of his homes, he is traveling. I am very glad for his success.

Dixon, my husband of nearly a quarter of a century (our twenty-third anniversary is in 2018), somehow scaled the top most walls of my lifelong solitude and independence. Like me, he has a nature that is aloof, yet loyal. He is not only a smart, well-read individual but one of the most genuine people I've ever met. He has a great sense of self and a wonderful sense of humor. He doesn't feel a need to prove anything to anyone. He came at me out of left field, and held on after a rejected first date, and somehow—to this day—everything works.

Other men who have impacted my life:

My plastic surgeon, Dr. Richard D'Amico, has been a consistently bright presence since I've had cancer. In 2008, I was a brand new, just-diagnosed traveler when I battled my way to his office at night, in a driving rainstorm. He was worth it.

Dr. D'Amico gets me—then and now. He listens to me. He has revealed his superb skills during my breast reconstruction and years of subsequent care. The night I first met him (when he agreed to see me—a stranger—right off the street), he was just back from an overseas trip to one of the poorest countries in the world, where he had performed plastic surgeries, free of charge, for suffering patients. Dr. D'Amico continues to be a true humanitarian and a compassionate human being. He performs surgeries without charging a dime over the insurance coverage, and he continues to bring healing and hope to the less fortunate, and to those deformed by illness and injuries, by performing greatly needed plastic surgeries all over the world.

When it comes to doling out admiration for my physicians, few make the cut. One of the few who does is Dr. Joe Contreras. He has been my pain management doctor since March 2017. Like Dr. D'Amico, he listens to me, cares about me, and doesn't use a stopwatch during our appointment time. He is committed to helping me manage my pain.

As I noted earlier, I have a unique relationship with Dr. Deena Graham, because she is the physician who gave me the news in November 2016 that I have stage IV metastasized cancer. In December 2017, we began trying new chemotherapy options. I appreciate her common sense, her humor, and her compassion. When she walks in the room, she always asks, "How are you doing?" or "I hear you aren't feeling very well."

My most recent reply, in December 2017:

"I need a new body!"

Her response: "Well, the reason I was late today is I was trying to *find* you a new body!"

Dr. Graham understands that quality of life supersedes length of life for me. Now that other treatments have failed, she is happy I am willing to at least try intravenous chemo, even though she knows the idea of putting such concentrated levels of poison in my body isn't something I want to do. But my life is on the edge and Dr. Deena is holding on to me, keeping me there. As our appointment ended she said, "I thank you for trusting me."

I cannot add anything more about this skilled physician than that.

****

A word about pain: In my life before cancer, I didn't think about it much, and I figured I had a pretty high threshold for pain. Childhood mishaps—breaks, sprains, and impacted wisdom teeth—never phased me, nor did the variety of adult operations that happened later. I never understood the narcotic pain epidemic in this country and always had a secret opinion that people were probably babying themselves when it came to pain.

Then, in November 2016, I learned I had been in Stage IV for nearly two years, (unknown to me) since February 2015. In March 2017, I learned the breast cancer had metastasized to my bones, ribs, chest wall, neck, spine, liver, skull, eye socket, and femur.

Now I understand what pain is. Indescribable. It has become as full-bodied and as much of a presence to me as any individual. When pain stands at my side, I can think of nothing else. My only hope—thank you, Dr. Joe—is to blunt the force of pain with another equally strong presence, and that is how I discovered dilaudid and fentanyl. These drugs, in the morphine family, are up to fifty times stronger than their other relatives. Their special characteristics are that they control pain while allowing me to function. Like trustworthy acquaintances, they support my life behind the scenes, while letting me live and be productive and enjoy life to its fullest. Pain is still there, but I can function.

Inevitably, the moment comes when these pain killers overstay their welcome, a fatigue and general loopiness kicks in, and I feel like a time traveler to another planet. In those moments, I'm apt to get questions like, "Are you high?" or "What kind of weed are you smoking?" (Sometimes followed by, "Can you get me some of what you have?")

St. Augustine is supposed to have said that "the greatest evil is physical pain." Now I understand.

****

Enough about pain. I want to think of someone who makes me happy, and so I think of Florian Bellanger.

Viewers of the Food Network and other shows of gastronomic derring-do will know Florian. He has been a judge for many years on Food Network's Cupcake Wars. He is an award-winning executive bakery chef and has been named among the "Ten Best Pastry Chefs in America". Born in Paris, Florian is recognized all over the world for his delicious creativity with pastry. His credits go on and on.

Well, I know Florian in a different way. He is my next-door neighbor.

We have become very close friends. I treasure his storytelling (he is one of the best), and I love the fact he keeps my French up to date. Dixon and I always look forward to his famous next-door barbecues, where we bump into guests who are, as often as not, among the world's most talented and famous chefs.

Florian has had a huge challenge in life. His wife died in 2011. She was working as a nurse in a New York hospital when she contracted a type of strep infection. Within forty-eight hours all her organs had shut down. She died, leaving Florian and their three young boys, ages seven, nine, and fourteen. We stepped up to help out with the boys, filling in whenever the family's Spanish nanny was unavailable. Florian travels a lot and needs the support back home. He co-owns an innovative pastry business in New Jersey called Mad-Mac, the purveyor of "The Authentic French Macarons and Madeleines." Needless to say, Florian makes the best macaroons, canelés, and madeleines—and his crepes are sublime. He began his career working with chocolate, and oh, when Florian indulges us with chocolate, there is nothing better! His various interests in the pastry business take him all over the world.

As for us, we feel most privileged when we are just hanging out in each others' backyards.

****

My highly unusual godparents: I have written about my godmother, Fleur Cowles (Aunt Fleur), a prominent editor, trend setter, and style celebrity of her day. Now, I want to take a long, loving look at my godfather, Peter Schoenberg, an Austrian-born nobleman, also known as His Serene Highness Prince Peter Schoenburg-Hartenstein.

My parents became friends with Prince Peter and his wife, Lee Russell Jones, when they all lived in Paris in the 1950s. My father was working for Look magazine, and Lee was working for the Magnum photo agency.

Uncle Peter (as I was told to call him) was born into an aristocratic family, in a time of gracious beauty and great privilege before the First World War. His father was ambassador to the Holy See, and Peter was born in Rome at the Austrian embassy. His mother, Princess Sophia Oettingen-Wallerstein, traced her noble lineage to before Charlemagne, as did the Schoenburgs. In the Congress of Vienna, the Schoenburgs were recognized as ranking equally with the ruling families of Europe.

After the collapse of the Austrian Empire in 1918, the Schoenbergs' fortunes changed, but Peter managed to carve out an exciting life between the two wars as a cavalry officer stationed in beautiful Vienna. After the war, Peter headed for South America and became an explorer on the Amazon. He eventually moved to America and with his wife, Lee, and quietly raised his American family of three children. His great passion was to help the unemployed in Harlem. He was so gracious, and so quiet about his aristocratic background, that no one would guess he came from a world of soaring castles and Viennese waltzes.

But one thing he could not hide—he was very handsome, tall, and imposing too. His demeanor was patient and kind, and he treated everyone he met as an equal, which—after all—is the sign of true nobility.

Uncle Peter died in 2003. By then, we had forged a wonderful bond through a few treasured meetings. I especially remember the dinners we shared at his favorite fine dining Italian restaurant, Scaletta, which was on the same block where he lived in New York City. Everyone knew him there, and he had his own favorite table. We could spend hours talking. It was one of those special friendships which crosses generational lines, where the younger person draws wisdom and guidance from the older. With age, Uncle Peter became less mobile, and I would visit him in his apartment in New York City, which was opposite the Museum of Natural History and

Central Park. His funeral, which I attended, was held at his home in upstate New York.

Oddly enough, a life that began at the height of aristocratic privilege ended in a most ordinary way: Uncle Peter died from complications of shingles. After he died, his wife wrote to say how much my visits meant to Peter in his last year of his life. What I remember today is an incredibly handsome, interesting, and charming Austrian prince, who made time for me and was always kind, affectionate, and complimentary toward me. So very different from my father!

****

Relatives, just a few: Samuel Korry was the only grandfather I ever met. He was born in 1895 in New York City, the son of Jewish immigrants from Vilna, Lithuania. Grandpa became a heart specialist and founded the American College of Cardiology. His wife, my grandmother, was also born from Jewish immigrants of Polish-Austrian-Hungarian background. She was an unusual woman, to say the least; most notably, she was a frustrated concert pianist who felt Grandpa ruined her chances of having a career. Sad to say but true—my grandmother was a very unhappy woman who thought of no one but herself. When the stock market crashed in 1929, my grandfather lost all his money, and she took to bed for a year. While bedridden, she listened to Father Coughlin, an anti-Semitic priest with a famous radio show. Under his influence, she became deeply anti-Jewish and made my grandfather cut off all contact with his brothers except for his brother Leo, who kept the family name, Korowitz—something my grandfather chose not to do.

My grandmother was a mystery to me, but my grandfather? I liked him very much. He was there for me during one of the most miserable experiences of my life, traveling to the dreaded Emma

Willard School in upstate New York. Grandpa would pick me up at the Port Authority Terminal, which was the last hop on my journey from Santiago Chile to JFK airport to the bus station. He was a short, bald headed, spectacled man, and I towered over him, even at age thirteen.

Grandpa was very kind to me. Each time he met me at the bus he'd take me to Schrafft's, a famous New York landmark. Schrafft's specialized in cakes, desserts, and light lunch fare—in that order. Grandpa always ordered a slice of cake for me. This famous Schrafft's cake was encircled with thin black chocolate mints. He got a kick out of the fact I would eat the mints and leave the cake. I think he enjoyed seeing me happy, even if it was only for a fleeting second.

Today, what I remember with some poignancy is Grandpa's views on cancer. Remember, he was a physician, and he was adamant about the future of cancer treatment. He told me that treatments had been developed for different cancers, but they would never see the light of day because they were all being shelved. Grandpa believed the medical profession was doing everything it could to stall cancer cures, because cancer was keeping the healthcare industry in business.

That's why, he said, I shouldn't expect a cure for cancer in my lifetime.

Some ironies are just too rich for a comment.

****

Favorite people from Dixon's family: Harp is the family name, and the line comes from old Southern stock. Dixon's grandfather (William Dixon Harp) served in the Confederate Army, 27th Georgia Regiment, Company C. After the war the family purchased a 400-

acre farm in the Garden Valley District of Macon County, Georgia, and Dixon's grandfather became a prominent planter who was interested in social, civic, and religious activities. The farm was—and is—a truly historic Southern destination of giant oaks, mulberry trees, and running streams. It has been in the family for a century and has been run for many years by Patty Rumph, Dixon's cousin, who is the daughter of Uncle Bud Harp.

The memories of Uncle Bud and his sister, Aunt Jenna, are especially dear to me. I treasure all of Dixon's family, but *especially* Uncle Bud and Aunt Jenna, who regarded me as their own. For a child who had been estranged from her own family, their presence in my life was an unexpected and cherished gift.

I got to know Dixon's family as my family right away, because in the first years of our marriage, Dixon and I spent unforgettable Christmases in Georgia, sitting on the front porch of the family home and gazing out at fields of cotton—a sweeter sight than all the December snow in the world.

Uncle Bud was one of the kindest and most genuine men I have ever met, and Aunt Jenna was a hoot—a lovely lady with a rakish sense of humor. She liked to kid me about Yankee accents (though she never accused me of having one) and was especially hard on the peculiar way Yankees pronounce pecan, with a long "e." (In Georgia, pecans are something like a national treasure, so Aunt Jenna must know.) "We don't eat pee-can pie," she would say. "A pee-can is something we put under our bed." No, in the South it's "puh-kahn." To this day, I add I laugh every time I hear someone say it the wrong way, and I tell them the Aunt Jenna story and Aunt Jenna's correct pronunciation. "Puh-kahn" it is!

Aunt Jenna's lively sense of humor was only one aspect of a deeply kind and thoughtful lady. The year after we were married,

Dixon and I were visiting for Christmas, when Aunt Jenna came into the kitchen one morning, holding a small object in her hand, which she offered to me.

"My mother, Dixon's grandmother, I'Ene, would want you to have this," she said, as she pressed into my hand her mother's wedding ring.

Dixon's grandmother was called I'Ene (short for Irene and pronounced "EYE-ene.") She was the true matriarch of the family, and Dixon was her favorite grandson. To be gifted with her wedding ring, especially from Aunt Jenna, was a moment of deep significance. To this day, when Dixon hears the name of his Grandmother I'Ene (who died in 1990 at age ninety-eight), he sheds a tear or too.

As for me, I had finally found my family.

****

Joe Trento: When my father was being sucked into the Chilean/Allende scandal, only one reporter, Joe Trento, took the time to probe the truth of the matter. The rest of the journalism herd simply assumed the worst about my father.

Joe Trento wasn't a flashy New York Times reporter, or a correspondent on a prestigious television program like 60 Minutes; no, at the time he worked for the Wilmington Delaware News Service. He felt the real story wasn't being told, that my father was being set up. So, he began diving into the mess. When he was done, he had not only proved my father's innocence, but he won awards for major reporting on the secret world of the CIA.

Later, Joe became a trusted friend of my father's, and his professional career has continued to climb on many fronts. He was the first correspondent to go to the front in the Iran-Iraq War. He's written eight books, including "The Secret World of the CIA". He pioneered non-profit journalism with his work at the Public Education Center, where he serves as president. At CNN, Joe produced documentaries such as the Merchants of War, and he continues his work as a producer and investigative journalist.

My father was a difficult man, but he did not deserve the sleight-of-hand injustices he was dealt at the hands of the government he was trying to serve. Thanks to the skill and tenacity of Joe Trento, my father was finally heard.

Lucky Girl

My godmother, Fleur Cowles, was a keen observer of things, which is why I never forgot what she wrote in 1971 to my mother:

"Deborah is such a perfect example of both you and Ed together," wrote Aunt Fleur. "One moment I look at her and I see Ed standing there, and the next moment I realize it is really Pat. Lucky girl."

****

How funny to be called a combination of my parents, when throughout my life I have had so little connection with either one! Still, it feels right to round out my book the way I began it, with Papa and Mummy. I've had minimal connection with my siblings too, but they have a place here as well, especially because in recent years there has been an evolution in our family dynamics.

That's why it would be wrong to leave a stark, coal-black, optic-white impression of my family relationships, especially my relationships with Papa and Mummy. It was so much more complicated than that. Throughout my life I tried, as best I could, to show them I cared. I went out of my way to do things for my father and mother right up until that difficult Christmas Eve, when an inconsequential moment flared into a confrontation and I chose to leave, rather than allow them to torment me again. Yet, even two years later, I was able to put all my personal feelings for them aside and do what any caregiver would do. I no longer had any emotional connection to them, so it was easy. I harbored no resentments or bad feelings. I was thankful for what they were able to give me and never focused on what they were unable to do.

In fact, being emotionally detached from my parents turned out to be a good thing. It gave me strength, independence, and a heightened awareness of what other people need.

Of course, just like in physical exercise, you only develop strength by pressing against resistance. As I have been going through old correspondences to write this book, I came across this note from my father, who never lost his instincts as a writer and journalist to express his ideas in print. His note reveals some of his thoughts about me and gives an idea of the resistance that helped to form me into the person I have become. When Papa wrote it in 1958, I wasn't even three years old:

> "Deborah is undoubtedly the most affectionate and cunning child we have had—that is, in the baby stages. But that is only as long as she is not crossed. Then the stubbornness inherited from both sides comes to view."
>
> And later, "Deborah, I'm afraid, cannot claim any prizes in this family—being the nuisance she is. She's put more weight on her face and has lost her fetching looks."

****

Clearly, Papa wasn't ignoring me. He was definitely observing me, and he had definite opinions about my progress. Maybe he recognized I came out of the womb too independent? That I would be difficult to control? In the high-powered world my parents lived in, they had to be able to control their environment and the people around them. Maybe there were subtler reasons too. At one point, right before he died, Papa told my brother Ted—almost as an aside (asides are wonderful places to drop clues to a mystery)—that things about me reminded him of his mother. Could that be why he didn't like me? But it wasn't my fault! But maybe that's why he kept me at a distance and showed dislike for me, right from the beginning.

In any case, my response—beginning in childhood—was to recognize I would have to build my own life, on my own terms. Until cancer, I have been able to do that with complete freedom.

So here is a rich irony:

My cancer, diagnosed in 2008, can be traced to the BRCA gene mutation, which I inherited directly from my father. This is something Papa would never know, because he died in 2003. Research has discovered that this gene mutation is concentrated in people of Eastern European Ashkenazi (Jewish) ethnicity—that is, my paternal ancestry. Carriers of this genetic anomaly have a higher incidence of cancer, especially breast and ovarian cancer.

As I will explain shortly, this information spurred me to reach out to my siblings in ways I never expected.

****

First, some thoughts about my mother. After Papa died in 2003, Mummy was lost— emotionally amputated. Her whole purpose for living was gone. Without a man in her life, she felt she had no life. Only a man could make her feel she was the center of everything. So, it wasn't surprising that, at my father's memorial service, she reconnected with one of Papa's best friends, Dick Witkin—and began a long, teenaged-like romantic relationship with him. Dick, the well-regarded New York Times writer, helped to finish my father's book, and he became my mother's focus in life.

However, Mummy carried over some habits from the past. In the years following Papa's death, she could not give up her high-spending ways. My father never made a lot of money, and any money he did make—or my mother inherited—they spent. Well, as it turned out, that spending engine had no off switch.

After Papa died, my mother started spending money at a furious rate, because Papa was no longer there to control it. I knew this because whenever she needed more money, or had overdrawn her account, I would be contacted either by Mummy or by one of her caregiver-secretaries. Ironically, it was because of my mother's spending habits that Alexandra and I first began an email relationship. Since Alexandra and my mother were not communicating directly with each other, I became the go-between for all of Mummy's caregiving and financial needs. Without Alexandra's financial support, Mummy would have nothing. We reconnected, not to rekindle a personal relationship, but strictly over my mother's needs.

For the twenty years after Papa's devastating turn of fortunes, Alexandra (a brilliant attorney and a Mergers & Acquisitions partner at a major firm) was the main financial support of our parents. Throughout our mother's widowhood, Alexandra continued that responsibility. She paid all of Mummy's expenses, including her caregiving, housing, taxes, and monthly bills, and she sweetened Mummy's bank account by subsidizing Papa's social security earnings.

But Mummy showed no respect for Alexandra's generosity. Rather than cut back on her spending, she simply had to spend more. And that was the way it stood for the rest of her life. Alexandra took care of our mother's financial needs, while I took care of her caregiving. I visited her regularly and managed her life; it was the role I assumed after my father died. Financially, Alexandra was a godsend. And that's how Alexandra and I choreographed our way through a difficult family situation.

In September 2017, at the age of ninety, Mummy passed away. After all the years of polite alienation, when this difficult, brilliant, wounding, incandescent presence passed out of my life—all I felt was relief. In less than a year, I had moved Mummy eight times—from home to hospital, then to an assisted living facility, then repeating those steps in a different configuration, and adding even more clinical settings as Mummy's life faded away.

Well, I had promised Papa on his deathbed that I would take care of Mummy, and I did.

Throughout Mummy's decline, she somehow kept alive the intense personal aura that drew so much attention throughout her life. Even in her waning years of activity, Mummy was something like a force of nature. She served as a docent with the Mint Museum, a cultural institution in Charlotte, and gave lectures on pottery and art through the Delhom Service League, the museum's highly regarded ceramics program.

Even as Mummy's life dimmed, her personality and will to dominate her surroundings did not. During that time, all she thought of was herself. She remained combative, sarcastic, self-centered, demanding, and self-serving. She didn't have a clue about the difficulties of my life or my cancer diagnosis, nor did she bother to ask about her children and grandchildren.

Still, I wanted to give Mummy her due. After she died, I gave a small memorial dinner in her honor, and invited her old friends from the Mint and the Delhom Service League, as well as close neighbors and the owner of Visiting Angels, who had provided me with the caregivers for the past ten years.

Mummy's last caregiver, Lisa, was there too. Thanks to her generous, joyous nature, Lisa never revealed all the many ordeals Mummy had put her through. How lucky I was to have found such a caring, loving, considerate person. Lisa was a real-life saver to me. She put up with Mummy's abusive ways and was my eyes and ears when I wasn't able to be in Charlotte. I will forever consider Lisa as family.

****

When I received the positive test results for the BRCA gene, I knew I had an ethical and moral responsibility to advise my siblings. Part of my learning curve into this disease was the knowledge that cancer targeted me because of the BRCA gene inherited through our father. Even though we were largely estranged and living separate lives, I felt obligated to alert my siblings to this genetic danger.

If we had been a close family, this news and the news of my cancer diagnosis would have been absorbed and dealt with right from the start, with everyone pulling together as a family unit. But in my family, where even the simplest gestures were made at arm's length, I knew this news would be disturbing. I also knew it had to be done.

I chose to begin by telling my brother Ted and my younger sister, Alexandra. Unlike our older sister Kelly, the three of us—Ted, Alexandra, and I—share obvious genetic markings, such as straight hair, similar coloring, and other physical characteristics.

In early March 2017, I received an email from Alexandra. She sent it at 5:45 a.m. as she was heading into surgery. She explained that a few days before she had been diagnosed with cancer and needed immediate surgery.

Here I was, the sister she hadn't wanted anything to do with, getting an email from her right before her cancer surgery! Was she reaching out for my help, for my support? Was it her way of acknowledging how I had helped to manage my mother's life for the past fourteen years, despite my personal feelings for my mother? Or perhaps she was trying to reach out to me, to acknowledge me as a compassionate, caring person? Or maybe she wanted to simply acknowledge that we faced a mutual enemy: cancer. In any case, that email devastated me. I was more upset about her cancer than my own.

Since then, things have continued to change between us. Despite a lifelong resistance to having me in her life, Alexandra has become very generous in her concern for me. For the first time since I've been diagnosed with cancer in 2008, she asks me regularly how I am doing. She has given me an opening to build something with her, and I cherish the opportunity. My whole life has been spent reaching out to help people; if I can finally help my own sister, and if I can convince her that she can count on me for anything—at any time—that would give me the greatest satisfaction. Now, we are connecting on a different level. I have even been out to visit her twice.

Since March 2017, Alexandra has endured extensive surgery, pain, discomfort, and chemotherapy, but she is cancer-free for now. We communicate every day. I hope in some way I am helping her.

I have also loved connecting with both Alexandra's daughters. Her youngest daughter, Sarah, whom I met for the first time in October 2017, is lovely. Her oldest daughter, Rebecca, whom I had a connection with for the first four years of her life, is now twenty-three and also lovely. Rebecca and I reconnected in December 2017 on one of her trips home from England, where she is studying under a Marshall Scholarship for a graduate degree. I so wanted children and would have loved to have been Auntie to Sarah and Rebecca all these years! I feel very blessed that I can finally be that auntie I always wanted to be.

The hard truth is, I have been given a short window to live (at least that's what my oncologist says), so I am glad that Alexandra and I have had this time. Of course, I hope for much more. It has given me peace to know that Alexandra does want a connection with me now and may even feel I have been of value in her life. All I know is I love her and want her to remain cancer-free. She has much to live for, not the least for her two wonderful daughters.

****

My older sister, Kelly is a cypher to me—a blank space. Whenever we have attempted family gatherings (like my father's memorial service in 2003, or a football weekend in Arizona, where Kelly lives), they have ended badly. For years, I went out of my way to do things for her, and later to do things for her daughter as well. It was never enough. Her constant grievances make me feel like I'm in a boxing ring, fighting shadows. Exhausting! Despite this, I felt an obligation to keep Kelly informed of Mummy's deteriorating health, which I did. Mission accomplished. Kelly may be a sister through blood but not in any other way. I will always wish Kelly and her daughter Christine well. I wish them nothing less than happiness, good health, and personal fulfillment.

It's just that I can't have them in my life.

****

My brother, Ted, is a different story altogether, though our brother-sister dynamic, until recently, was just as complicated.

He's known as Ted, Teddy, Edward, or Eduardo, depending on who knew him when, and his many names are a testament to all the many places he's been and the things he's done, which include graduating from the University of Chicago and living in Egypt. He speaks French and German, as well as some Arabic and Spanish. There are definite echoes of my father in his eclectic interests and independent lifestyle, though he is a much more giving and sensitive person than my father, and—unlike my father—family is very important to him.

Ted (as I call him) is the only boy in the family. I was twenty-two months younger, and only wanted to follow him around. I was the adoring kid sister. Then he went off to boarding school. My parents considered him the jewel in the family crown, and they sent him to two of the most prestigious schools in England, St. Peter's Court and Harrow.

In 1970, when I was fourteen, Ted came home to Chile on one of his regular holidays from Harrow. He was no longer the nerdy, somewhat portly prep-school kid in a stiff school uniform—he had become a living embodiment of the late '60s. I hardly recognized him with long hair, a mustache, dark sunglasses, bell bottoms, a pink tuxedo shirt, and an off-white sheepskin vest! All of a sudden, Ted was six inches taller and all grown up. For the first time in years, he looked cool to me (though not so cool to my parents).

I set him up with Joyce, one of my girlfriends, who had been a runner-up contestant for the title of Miss Chile. Although Ted had done everything he could to shed his preppie, English boarding school image, to Joyce he was forever the image of the romantic movie hero. She called him Preppie just like Ali MacGraw called Ryan O'Neill in Love Story, which was the big movie of the year.

After graduating from the University of Chicago, Ted went to

Egypt to live for a time. When he returned to the USA, he joined Johnson & Wales University, the century-old, private nonprofit university well known for its culinary arts program. Ted worked his way up the ranks, first as Food & Beverage Director to eventually Chair of the Beverage and Dining Service Department at the University in Providence, Rhode Island. He joined the faculty in 1983 and led the creation of the school's beverage programs where he teaches wine courses. Ted earned many certifications over the years: Certified Specialist of Spirits (CSS) and Certified Wine Educator (CWE) through the Society of Wine Educators (SWE), and he's a Certified Hospitality Educator (CHE).

Ted has sat on the executive committee of many well-known wine and beverage societies. For example, the US Bartenders' Guild Master Accreditation Program, Maitre de Table Restaurateur, and Echanson Provincial of La Chaine des Rotisseurs. He is a certified Bordeaux Wine Educator and has the title of Formador Homologado del Vino de Jerez. Ted is passionate about wine, traveling to vineyards and teaching others, and naturally passionate about cooking and pairing wines with food.

For most of his rise in the beverage world, we communicated—but not in a personal or meaningful manner. We rarely saw each other. Ted has three sons: Alex, Ben, and Jon. I found it difficult to form relationships with them, no matter how much I tried. Ted and his wife at the time had little interest in my being Auntie to their children. But we did stay in touch, and I did witness what a wonderfully involved and caring father he was to his sons. He did all the things our father never did—nor, for that matter, do many fathers. Ted actually spent time with his kids! He was an involved father. He took on all the traditional roles of a mother—cooking, bathing, and exposing them to good foods and foreign lands. And always, always—he made time for them!

As we all know, time isn't just the passage of moments; it can also heal and restore. In the last year, I have formed a good relationship with Ted's youngest son, Jon, and I have reestablished communication with Ben, his middle son, who also happens to be my godson. As of this writing, a relationship with Alex is still a question mark, but I will always wish him well. Dixon and I were close to Alex until he graduated from Ohio State Law School. As for the future? We shall see, and in the meantime, we wish him well—always.

For much of our lives, I just didn't fit in. Ted and I had nothing in common. I detected no interest in Ted that had to do with me or anything I was doing.

Then two things happened: Our mother became ill and cancer came back to me with a vengeance. As had happened with Alexandra, the reality of cancer and the illness of our remote and distant mother brought us closer. Probably more important, Ted made changes in his personal life that began to make room for me as well.

In 2016, I was planning a small birthday party for our mother, who was turning ninety that year. Her birthday party had become an annual event that I had planned for about the previous six years. I wanted to hold the party in her condo in Charlotte, North Carolina, where she was living at the time.

To my happy surprise, Ted contacted me to say he wanted to throw the party with me, and we agreed to meet in Charlotte.

It was the first time I had seen Ted in seven years. We didn't spend much time together because of our schedules—I arrived Saturday morning from New Jersey and the party was Saturday night. Early Sunday morning, Ted was flying back to his home in Rhode Island.

As fate would have it, shortly after Ted left on Sunday, our mother collapsed, and I found myself calling 911 and racing Mummy to the hospital.

If I had I not been there, she would have died. As it was, the crisis marked the beginning of her demise. From this point on, she never went back to living in her condo or living alone. Of course, I emailed the news to Ted immediately, and—once again—crisis was transforming a sibling relationship. Ted and I started communicating more closely and compassionately.

Then one day, I received a letter from Ted that meant everything to me. He greeted me as Debritu, the lovely name I was called in Ethiopia by my friends, though Ted was the only one in our family ever to use it. I cherish the name and the very sound of it, which is endearing and personal.

"Hola Debritu,

Thanks for being such a good sister and daughter to Mummy. She didn't deserve all you did for her, especially after the way she treated you so many years ago.

I wish that over the years we had been able to maintain the same relationship as we have now, but hopefully you now understand what the constraints to that were. I'm glad that we can communicate in the meaningful way we do … your generous reaching out to both Alexandra and Kelly are a reflection of your good human nature."

Then he talked about Mummy, then in her final decline.

"I don't wish Mummy anything but a lack of discomfort and pray that my final days are nothing like hers," Ted wrote. "She was always a fighter and the way she is struggling now reflects that … she seemed so different to me when growing up, and I understand what the loss of Papa meant to her, but she wasn't able—when we were kids—to balance her husband and her own needs with having children. As Papa said, they probably shouldn't have had kids. But, we—or at least I—had an amazingly opportunistic childhood, thanks to them both. And for those experiences and memories, I am eternally grateful."

I was moved to read these thoughts, which I had expressed for years and were now being echoed by my brother.

Ted closed his letter to me this way:

"Anyway, enough of my pontificating. I really wanted to just say thank you."

Ted's letter brought tears to my eyes. It may have taken us a long time to finally have a brother-sister relationship, but we finally have one. For that I am so grateful. I do love him!

Ted's letter made me realize once again that I, like my brother, am eternally grateful to Papa and Mummy for the life they gave me. The sheer wonder of growing up in Ethiopia and Chile is as fresh today as it was five decades ago. We were extremely lucky to have the opportunities they gave us. To have experienced diplomats and politicians as ordinary visitors in our living room has always given me a sense of proportion about fame, privilege, and power that is healthy and good. It was a life that made me strong and intuitive. And following me everywhere is the special gift I was given in Ethiopia that is with me to this day: often, when I encounter a stranger, I recognize a friend.

Yes, as Aunt Fleur said, I *am* a lucky girl. It has been an incomparably wonderful thing to be the ambassador's daughter.

ACKNOWLEDGEMENTS

Over the years several people encouraged me to write a book, but the timing was never right. There is an old saying attributed to both the Talmud and to Jose Marti, the Cuban revolutionary and poet. It goes something like this: "A man hasn't truly lived until he's had a son, planted a tree, and written a book." That has stuck with me all these years. Although I had several miscarriages and didn't produce a son, I've spent a lifetime both personally, and in my career choices, taking care of other people as if they were my children, sisters, brothers, or parents. They have been "my children"—"my sons." I've planted several trees in several different continents that all bloom at different times of the year, a constant reminder of nature's ability to change and survive no matter how harsh the weather or storm may be.

And now I've written my book, a book about a girl who grew up differently than most American children but who nonetheless has experienced what so many of us do in our quest for survival. I was fortunate to have been born to two journalists who had an interest in the world and who taught me to see life as bigger than just myself.

I want to thank my husband, my friends, former colleagues, strangers, and anyone who ever stood by me, believed in me, and nourished me. Curiosity, they say, is man's best index to freshness. I continue to be curious about everything and everyone.

Finally, I want to thank Mark Graham for introducing me to Jean Torkelson. Her patience, dedication, passion, expertise, and interest in helping me bring my story to light in the way I envisioned it has been more than a blessing. She helped me shape my story into the kind of book I wanted to share with others—and in the process has become a good friend. I am forever grateful to her.

Made in the USA
Middletown, DE
22 March 2018